THE FARM

Treasure Remembered

Evelyn Whitfield

PREMIERE EDITIONS INTERNATIONAL, INC.
CORVALLIS, OREGON

About the Cover Art

The hooked rug depicted on the front cover is one of the large family collection of hand-hooked rugs and wall-hangings made by Ethel (Peggy) Allworth between 1932 and 1972. This original rug design is a true "primitive" created in the style of Grandma Moses reflecting the beauty and simplicity of The Farm.

The farm home on the back cover is an original watercolor painting by Nancy Allworth. The cover design is the work of Karen Freeman.

THE FARM

Treasure Remembered

Evelyn Whitfield

PREMIERE EDITIONS INTERNATIONAL, INC.
CORVALLIS, OREGON

All photographs, drawings, documents, media clippings and memorabilia used as illustration are from the Allworth, Walker and Whitfield family scrapbooks, except as noted. Extracts from the journal of Ethel (Peggy) Allworth are included in this story.

Also by Evelyn Whitfield ~
Three Year Picnic:
An American Woman's Life Inside Japanese
Prison Camps in the Philippines During WWII

PREMIERE EDITIONS INTERNATIONAL, INC.
2397 NW Kings Blvd. #311, Corvallis OR 97330
(541) 752-4239 ~ FAX (541) 752-4463
E-Mail: *publish@premiere-editions.com*

Visit our Web Site:
www.premiere-editions.com

Editors: Irene L. Gresick, Beatrice Stauss

Contributing
Writers: Jodie Allworth, Nancy Allworth,
                      Gail Cornelius, Katharine Ewalt,
                      Linden Hagood, Lea Lutz,
                      Ted Hollingsworth, Peggy Sedlacek,
                      Lauri Watkins

Illustrators and
Designers: Nancy Allworth, Jodie Allworth,
                      Karen Freeman

Library of Congress Control Number: 2001087108
ISBN: 1-891519-08-5
First Edition
Printed in the United States of America

Dedicated to the
Family
and to farm folks everywhere

NEE · TEMERE · NEE · TIMIDE

Allworth

*"The Lord is the portion of my inherit-
ance and of my cup: thou maintainest
my lot. The lines are fallen unto me in
pleasant places; yea, I have a goodly
heritage."*

—Psalms 16:5

Acknowledgments

This book could not have been written without the generous contributions of family members and friends who worked with me: my sister Peggy's daughters Jodie and Nancy Allworth; their daughters Katharine Ewalt, Lea Lutz, Linden Hagood, and Peggy Sedlacek; my daughter Lauri Watkins; and Ted Hollingsworth, a friend.

The totally unselfish dedication of my publisher and editor, Irene Gresick, who also created most of the format, and Bea Stauss, whose incredibly discerning eye catches even the tiniest of errors, have been essential.

The photographs were found in the many family scrapbooks. Nancy and Jodie both added much with their excellent sketches.

Gail and Grant Cornelius, the present owners of the Farm, have extended the most gracious hospitality to us, and wrote the final chapter.

Prologue

It meant so many things to so many people! To Jodie, it was the whole of <u>home</u>, the only completely *satisfying and enduring one* for her. For Nancy, it was her *idyllic childhood.* For Norman and me, The Farm was the *refuge* after war-torn years of prison and privation, the place of plenty and peace. For Ethel, The Farm was her canvas, on which she could create her richness of bright beauty. For Ed, it was his *dream* come true, his vision of what needed to be. *For all the children, it was heaven. This was no ordinary place to live. This was The Farm!*

This is a tale told by many voices, blended together in a song of love. Where there are no quotation marks, the voice is my own. I will give each other voice the floor by calling his or her name, so you will always know who is talking. The principal speakers are my two nieces, Jodie and Nancy Allworth, and I have chosen many excerpts from the rich journal of their mother, Ethel (Peggy) Allworth, my sister. The story spans four generations, including the grandparents, and the time is from 1932 to 1972. I did not attempt to keep it in chronological order — some events in life happen just once, or suddenly — some over a long span of time, and events are not viewed exactly the same by any two people.

The Farm Families

Ed & Ethel (Peggy) Allworth, husband and wife
and their four children:
Edward, Jodie, Kent, and **Nancy**
Grampa Walker,
Ethel and Evelyn's father
Grandad Allworth,
Ed Allworth's father
Evelyn & Norman Whitfield,
Ethel's sister and brother-in-law, and
Lauri Watkins, their daughter
Edith Allworth Metcalf, Ed Allworth's sister,
and her daughters:
Lois, Celia, Ann, and **Delores**
Jodie Allworth's children:
Linden, Lea, Gay, Ralph,
and **Peggy (Little Peg) Majors**
Nancy Allworth's children:
Mark, Katherine, Karen, and **Kent Ewalt**
Edward Allworth's son:
Clark

Other Family Members in the Story:

Dorothy (Dot) and **Otto Pick**, Ethel and Evelyn's
sister and brother-in-law
Wyn (Windy) and **Mary Walker**, Ethel and
Evelyn's brother and sister-in-law

Ethel (Peggy) Allworth

Table of Contents

PART I:
THE BEGINNING

    1. Dream Realized ~17
    2. Making a House a Home ~ 23
    3. The Propert ~ 25
    4. Ed & Ethel ~ 29
    5. Rugs ~ 33
    6. The Wonderful Barn ~ 39
    7. Jodie Remembers ~ 43
    8. Babies ~ 53

PART II:
GROWING UP

    9. Nancy & Kent ~ 57
  10. The Dairy ~ 61
  11. Grampa Walker ~ 65
  12. Upstairs ~ 67
  13. Attic Room ~ 71
  14. Downstairs ~ 75
  15. Parents ~ 80
  16. Guests ~ 83
  17. Work in Progress ~ 85
  18. Water ~ 89
  19. Bees ~ 94
  20. Work Horses ~ 97

PART III:
LIFE ON THE FARM

  21. Bountiful Harvest ~ 107
  22. Cooking ~ 109
  23. Horses ~ 113
  24. Help ~ 120
  25. Evelyn ~ 123

26. Dot's Wedding ~ 125
27. Grandad ~ 127
28. Sayings ~ 129
29. The Fire ~ 130
30. Homecoming ~ 133
31. Model A ~ 137
32. Christmas ~ 143
33. Buggies ~ 153
34. Cockers ~ 155
35. The Little Rocking Horse ~ 159
36. Hats ~ 160
37. Ted ~ 161
38. Nancy ~ 165
39. Trees and Garden ~ 171
40. Climate ~ 179
41. The War Years ~ 181
42. Kent ~ 186

PART IV:
A NEW GENERATION

43. Linden ~ 191
44. Lea ~ 195
45. Gay ~ 199
46. Lauri ~ 201
47. Second Visit ~ 215
48. Peggy ~ 217
49. Katharine ~ 221

PART V:
THE END OF AN ERA

50. Tomorrow ~ 227
51. Deciding to Move ~ 229
52. Cornelius ~ 231

EPILOGUE ~ 237
INDEX ~ 241

Courtesy of A.C. Waling, Lithography, Portland, OR

PART I:

THE BEGINNING

Farm Residence of Caleb Davis; Erected 1878, 4 miles S.W. of Corvallis, Oregon

CHAPTER 1

Dream Realized

My beautiful sister Ethel, preparing dinner in her big, bright kitchen on Park Terrace Drive in Corvallis, Oregon, startled, looked up in total amazement as her husband—this quiet man—burst into the room almost shouting with excitement: "Peg, I think I've found it!" (Ethel was always known to her husband and friends as "Peggy.")

She knew "it" had to be a farm. They had been talking *farm*, dreaming of owning and living on a real farm, raising their children on a farm. Ed was born and raised on a farm, and had always longed for that life again. Through the long years of WWI and after, weary years that included coming home, wounded from the war, getting started all over again, marriage, fatherhood, years on crutches and riding a streetcar in Portland to work, this was his Shangri-la.

"As the crow flies," the Farm lies fifty miles east of the Pacific Ocean. Mary's River runs along the lower, eastern, edge. There are two ranges of mountains, the Cascades to the east and the Coast Range to the west, standing guard near enough to be seen and admired but not near enough to close it in. It is literally in the very heart of a richly fertile, pristinely beautiful, farm and forest valley—the Willamette Valley. The climate is mild, frequently damp, seldom very cold or hot, not often producing lightning and thunder or destructive storms. Summers are delightful in this region. Winters seem long under gray skies and dark nights, for it in the northern sector, but yet snow is a rare treat. Spring and Fall are radiantly beautiful in the whole valley, from the

Columbia River to California. There are trees everywhere —
city streets are lined with them, hills and mountains are
covered with them; they border highways and cling to the
rocky slopes. Fields are rice-paddy green even in winter.

Wild creatures abundantly inhabit the hedgerows and
trees of the Farm. The Calapooya Indians left their
arrowheads and relics along the river as memorials of their
long-ago occupancy. This Farm is a lovely jewel in a perfect
setting. Its beginnings and its history are modest, even
humble, and it was a classic example of its time.

"What he had found sounded too good to be true," Ethel
wrote in her journal, "but right after dinner that night he
took me and the children out to see his find — 106 acres about
five miles southwest of Corvallis, with a large house built in
1878 and a wonderful big old barn. There were other
buildings, too — a stone house for storing fruit and
vegetables, a long grape arbor, a granary and pump house,
and a sheep shed with a pigeon loft on top. There was a little
District School and a community church nearby."

Bob Lynn/Gazette-Times

(Above) The Caleb Davis House, at 3375 S.W. 53rd St., was
built around 1879. An etching of the same house (below)
shows the several barns included on the homestead.
Illustration from D.D. Fagan's "History of Benton County," 1885

Courtesy of Corvallis Gazette-Times July 1, 1988

All the years away from the country, this "farm boy" had itched to get back to farming, and was always watching for just the right place. Ethel joined his dream, simply because he wanted it so. In 1932, Western Oregon and the rest of the United States had sunk into a severe economic depression that changed the lives of every family on a moderate income. Ed—Major Edward Christopher Allworth—was the sole support of this family, and was seeing his salary from the Oregon Agricultural College sink to an alarmingly low figure. With several dependents already, and a growing family, and somewhat hampered by his own limiting physical disability from football and war injuries, he was troubled by what seemed to be an uncertain future.

Ed was a renowned WWI hero, a Medal-of-Honor winner, but he was reti-

cent, humble, and always conscientious. He was a devoted and charmingly loving husband, a somewhat stern father, and an outstanding citizen. Ed was the Manager of the Memorial Union—the student union—on the OAC campus, and the Alumni Secretary. He had a major part in the money raising for that building, at a time when the economy was so bad that sometimes the pledges made by even loyal alumni might be as small as five dollars. A bronze bust of him is on a pedestal in the lounge at the MU, and one of the large meeting rooms bears his name and has a wall dedicated to his memory. He was at one time, before his retirement, considered to be the dean of student union managers in the nation, and he was honored by this university with a Doctor of Philosophy degree, so was entitled to use the title "Doctor." But Ed was widely known and almost universally addressed and spoken of as "The Major," for his distinguished WWI record, his military bearing, and his patriotic activities. A handsome man, somewhat shy and hard to know, he could be sentimental and romantic, and never ceased to woo his pretty and beloved wife.

Although his position at the college was important and respected, the compensation at that time was incredibly low, and in 1932 seemed on the verge of disappearing altogether, as the finances for the Memorial Union project were so uncertain. After his return from the War, he had worked for a period of time in Portland as a bookkeeper, and it was from that job that he had been lured back to Corvallis in 1925 to work for the college, a move that was happy for everyone but me—I was heartbroken to leave Rose City Park School and my friends, and the prospect next year of attending Grant High School, which had just opened. I loved Portland then, and still do, but Corvallis is my birthplace and my beloved "home town," so I am grateful for the "larger plan."

Because he truly was also an experienced farmer, Ed's decision to move his family from their large home, a former fraternity house at the edge of the campus, to the country, where land had been decreasing steadily in price, seemed wise and timely. He could trade his town property for part of the cost of the rural home and acreage. On a farm, there would be some government supports and tax-deductible expenses. He knew they could raise almost everything needed to feed this burgeoning family, and they could more graciously survive the threat of difficult times ahead.

In 1932, the family, with two young children, Edward and Jodie, Grampa Walker, and me, little sister Evelyn, would be spaciously accommodated. The time seemed right, and the move was made, and a family tradition came into being. Many family and non-family members were to sleep in those narrow-windowed bedrooms. There were siblings of all ages, nephews and nieces, aunts, grandparents, homeless kids, two more children born after the move, and

countless friends. There was always room, and welcome, and there were memorable holiday celebrations and meals and picnics—celebrations of birthdays, graduations, home-comings, and honors.

Old walls came down to make new rooms, and with every change, the charm of the country home, its dignity and grace, was enhanced. Music was there and the songs of young voices, sorrow and hard work, warm and delicious meals, laughter and tears, heartbreak and fulfillment. A neighbor family friend, Dr. Tom Wolfe, once said to Jodie many years later: "Your parents' home was an island paradise, and there are none like it."

Jodie describes her first impression on that visit: "We went into the kitchen just to the left. Joe Basselin, the owner, was shaving from a pan of water heated on a wood stove. The only light was from a kerosene lamp. The doorway out of the kitchen was covered with blankets hung to keep the heat in the room. I noticed that there were small bedrooms behind the living room fireplace, also with blankets hung over the doorways. It all seemed very mysterious to me at the time—exciting—not fearsome!"

Ethel's journal records vividly, "Mr. and Mrs. Basselin were generous and encouraged us to wander, which we did. It certainly was challenging!

"In the house there was no heat except from fireplace fires; no telephone, no electricity, no inside plumbing. It didn't matter; we loved it, talked it all over, and decided to do it. Then it wasn't long before we traded our home on Park Terrace for the Farm on SW 53rd and actually moved." With stars in their eyes, they moved almost immediately.

The asking price was $15,000, and it would take Ed sixteen years to pay out the sum. Jodie takes up the story: "I was very small when I went along with my parents to look at the Farm. As we drove up the lane, the great old house on the top of the hill appeared unpainted and naked, surrounded by bare fields. We entered at the back door through a yard overgrown with grasses and weeds, and surrounded by a paintless picket fence. A grape arbor, wild with untrimmed vines and tendrils, led to the porch, which ran the length of the back of the house."

Ethel joins in, "As soon as we were a little bit settled, we started the huge renovation. First, we had a furnace installed. It had hot water coils to circulate the heat throughout the house in radiators. We hired a carpenter, good friend Mr. Kammerer, a neighbor when we lived on Kings Road, tall, lanky, kind — to help us. He looked it all over, pondered, and told us what we could and couldn't do. He took out partitions in the living room that had walled off the two small bedrooms, creating a wonderful large room with a fireplace free-standing in the middle, and he built in beams where the partitions had been, and bookshelves on the walls. The narrow, steep stairs, winding up out of the living room, had a solid front wall which we had removed and replaced with an open stair rail."

Jodie says she called Mr. Kammerer "Mr. Carpenter," thinking that was his name, of course, since everyone said "the carpenter." "He worked many long hours. I loved the sawhorses. I made string harnesses for them when they weren't being used, to make them look like the work teams. And I became very 'wealthy' in *coins* as the electrical boxes went up. It was some time before I found out they weren't real money — I didn't really know *money* at all."

CHAPTER 2

Making a House a Home

Electricity and plumbing were installed, and a country party-line telephone. Our *ring* was 'five short rings' at first—later, it was a long and a short. Each neighbor had a

special ring, and we'd crank out the rings to make a call. It was 'one ring' to get the operator. Everyone heard everyone else's rings, so you didn't want to give away any secrets over the line—you might be telling the entire neighborhood. (I believe Peggy told me there were nine families on that little rural telephone line.) Most of the time all was discreet unless someone heard your ring and just happened to want to tell you something on the spur of the moment, while you were already on the line." Ed had a modern drainboard and a stainless-steel double sink put in the kitchen. Mr. Kammerer built fire escapes out of two upstairs bedrooms.

On the first floor were two fireplaces. A single chimney served both the kitchen woodstove and the dining room fireplace. The large dining room opened from the living room, and glass doors were added there eventually to keep the heat in the dining room during the winter months of the war. The doors were otherwise open so that there was room for everyone when we were all gathered together. The dining room had two glass-fronted corner cabinets which through the years were filled with exquisite crystal goblets, Spode china, a gold-banded dinner set inherited from Jackie Horner, an elegant silver coffee service, and a large collection of lovely friendship tea cups.

Ethel remembers that during the first winter the curtains blew out into the rooms. So storm windows were installed, and every time a wall was opened, insulation was poured in.

"Usually Mr. Kammerer worked alone on the renovating and restoring of this fine old house. Much later on we had the help of our handy-man, Harris Whitby ('Whispering Harry,' we all called him, because the dear little man never spoke in a normal tone — you had to listen!). The process began with tearing out the bedrooms behind the fireplace, then stuccoing the fireplace, papering, painting, scrubbing, and cleaning. When the house was wired for electricity, Professor Ridenour, from the OAC Foundry Department, fashioned the chandeliers out of wrought iron to look like rustic candelabra. Professor Ridenour was a family friend and had been a neighbor back in the days when Grampa Walker's family lived on South 13th Street. Beautiful hand-hewn beams were put where the partitions had been, and bookshelves on the walls. It was now a large and stately living room ready for the many guests to come."

CHAPTER 3

The Property

The Farm was shaped a bit like a parallelogram. As was often the case in farms of that era, it was long and narrow after the style of old French properties around New Orleans, where each one needed access to a stream or river, so were arranged accordingly. A slanting county road bordered it on the west-northwest, and on the east, a winding river—Mary's River—said to have been named for the first white woman to cross it, Mary Lloyd, circa 1846. The Ingles and Basselins bordered us on the northeast and south. Across the road on the west lived the Larson family, with raucous turkeys!

To the northwest lay a large patch of scrub oak and blackberry brambles on the southern extreme of the Alnutt place. (That farm was later acquired by the Allworth family.) The open field in the far west of the Farm had not been cleared of the many oak stumps, so it was quite unusable except as goat pasture! That area also suffered from the

further blight of a large, spreading section of Canadian thistle, extremely difficult to eradicate. Even the goats wouldn't eat those thistles!

It was to take years of back-breaking work to clear and clean up these areas, but it was finally accomplished. Ed probably recognized that in the beginning, but it must have seemed to him just part of the challenge, for he never hesitated. His father had homesteaded in southern Washington, carving out of the wilderness a home place for his large family. There they had picked up rocks to clear the fields, sometimes eight hours a day. Jodie remembers: "Dad told me stories about helping his father break horses for the Cavalry, as another source of income for that family. Their cows on that large farm were free to roam and hard to find in the tall ferns—they just seemed to know when to come home, and they wore bells around their necks."

The western section on the Farm became a beautiful grain field. Sometimes rye grass was grown there, sometimes wheat. Jodie never liked having it be put to rye grass, "because after harvesting the farmer burned the field, which was ugly, polluting, and always a bit worrisome."

Before the improvements began on the house, the old picket fence was in poor shape. In some places, it was down and most of it was inundated with myrtle (a vine with a small blue flower somewhat like a morning glory, and the

vine never stops!). One of the big jobs was pulling and hacking out the roots of the myrtle so the fence could be straightened up, restored, and painted. Old pictures show the fence all around the front and back yards, so the best panels were set up across the front of the side yard to the back of the yard, and painted white. The battle with the myrtle continued through the years. At that early time, other than the myrtle, the only flowers on the place were the occasional old-fashioned daffodils.

Corvallis Gazette-Times, Corvallis Ore., Friday, July 1, 1988

• Historic county homes

Caleb Davis House

■ Built around 1879. 3375 S.W. 53rd St. Farmhouse with milkhouse. Residence.

Caleb Davis sought his fortunes in the gold fields of California. He settled in Corvallis in 1870 and opened a granary in partnership with Joseph Avery. After three years, he sold his interest and bought the Hiram Allen Donation Land Claim.

The farmhouse has about 4,000 square feet of living space. It was constructed with hand-made iron nails and hand-hewn timbers. It features four bedrooms upstairs and a greenhouse on the second story. A stone fireplace rises up the middle of the living room.

Davis farmed and raised stock, and was known for his carpentry skills. He served two terms as Benton County commissioner, from 1880 to 1884.

Courtesy Corvallis Gazette-Times, July 1, 1988

CHAPTER 4

Ed & Ethel

Jodie says, "Dad was very humble about his accomplishments and successes, and totally grateful for the favor and abundance God brought him and his family. He never hesitated to help others in need and he felt were deserving. It was not charity to him—just the way things were done. It was a long time before we children came to realize how much effort it took to provide for the extra people in the home. We just thought it was fun to have a full house, and our parents would not have it any other way.

Aunt Edith, Dad's older sister, with her four daughters, came and stayed at different times; Nancy says she was too young so didn't get to know these cousins as well as she would have liked, but each was definitely cherished 'family'." Jodie and Delores, being about the same age, became fast friends and buddies.

Nancy explained that her mother told her one time that Ed didn't know how to show love to his children except by working with them, and teaching them the right way to do things. He was sometimes deeply amused. Once at the dinner table, when Jodie was very small, she did not like his admonition about something, and shook her tiny fist at him. He chuckled and let the matter drop! Ahead of his time, he was very supportive of his girls in their interests, never recognizing limitations for them. We girls always thought that Ethel was not in full agreement with his encouragement of this attitude, as she felt strongly that a woman's place was as wife and mother above all else.

Her career was home-making, nurturing. She was conservative and sentimental. Her vitality and energy carried her through strenuous days. Ethel was interested and active in politics, national and local affairs. But careers were not something she really wanted for her girls at all. Jodie and I agree with Nancy. Ethel did a wonderful job of training her daughters, and me, for home-making and child-raising. She tolerated my teaching, thinking of it as important and as following in our father's footsteps, but I know she expected me to stay at home after Lauri was born. I did, for the pleasure of it, but as soon as my child went to school, so did I. Our other sister, Dorothy (Dot), had a long and successful career as a private secretary, and sometimes Ethel rather wistfully remarked that she thought Dot and I were so much smarter than she, because she had <u>never worked</u>! Of course, we told her over and over that she had worked much harder than we, and that her work was more important than anything. She was, in our opinion, the absolute ultimate as a mother and home-maker.

Nancy and Jodie also had both—Nancy has four children, and Jodie five. They also had careers. Nancy became a landscape architect, an accomplished musician, a college instructor, and an artist. Jodie raised blooded horses, and ran a ranch in Eastern Washington. She is a talented painter, as well.

Jodie's Family

Nancy's Family

Courtesy Tom Warren, Photographer
Corvallis Gazette-Times, December 1969

CHAPTER 5

Rugs

Ethel's journal: "One of my favorite projects and probably the most useful was making primitive hooked and braided rugs. We couldn't afford to buy floor covering for that big house. Making them was <u>so</u> enjoyable, and I covered the floors, stairs, and walls. During the anxious war years, if I hadn't had my rugging, I would have had a very hard time staying happy. I learned that work is love made visible.

I set up my rug frame back of the living room fireplace; heard many interesting things and nice music on the radio back there, and could see the children come up the lane from school in the afternoon. The babies played back there, and while I rugged sometimes I supplied the sound effects for their games. Busy times — I loved every minute of it."

The fireplace in the dining room had a hundred-year-old octagon-barrel flintlock rifle under the carved wooden

mantel. Ethel wrote, "Over the fireplace, I lettered: *Who hath a home, a heart, a cheery fire, hath sweet content, for these are heart's desire.* It spoke for all of our family." She also painted and richly decorated wood fire screens that were made especially for both the dining room and living room fireplaces. Those screens cut the cool draft when the fires were not lit.

Ethel made a priceless hooked rug for the narrow stairway, which had a bend near the bottom and one near the top, with the history of our country colorfully depicted from Columbus at the very bottom to the space age on the upper landing. Each step showed an important era, each riser the next one. Because it was custom made for that stairway, it is still in place, carefully preserved by the Corneliuses, who live there now. Hundreds of people over the years have looked at it, treasuring its unique value.

Ethel's rugs were nearly always her own design, with deep rich colors from the dye pot, and they were meant for the ages, closely hooked and carefully backed with strong material. She found many ideas from greeting cards, paintings, fabric designs, magazine ads and pictures, and most of all from her own creative inspirations. Many of the materials were given her—old, torn, moth eaten, faded, but in her hands they became lustrous with color. I was with her when a friend gave her two old wool flannel sheets, and she was ecstatic!

Jodie tells: "In a huge basket, she saved all of the buttons, fasteners, zippers and pins to use in other ways. All of the buttons that were removed from her heaps of used clothing rug rags went into the "button basket." The basket was about a three-gallon capacity, and was two-thirds or more full of buttons of every size and description most of the time. This made a marvelous toy/babysitter. She would spread a sheet on the floor in the room where she was working, and together we would dump that amazing collection onto the sheet. Hours were spent sifting and sorting, organizing sets of buttons. Sometimes we found one or two fancy old Victorian buttons, but eventually all of those were removed for her collection, or given away."

Ethel made two very large, room-sized rugs. During World War II, she finished one for the dining room. And after the war she made the Allworth rug, the family crest, bordered by dogwood blossoms and other Canadian motifs for the living room. (Ed's father was born in Ontario, Canada.) It took several men to help her move the rug when

it came time to change it on the frame. An enormous amount of material went into this rug, and old army socks, donated to her for this purpose, were a large part of the bulk.

Many of the rugs were designed to be hangings for the walls—superbly detailed flying geese, richly colored harvest scenes, family crests, landscapes, flowers, autumn leaves, Grandma Moses style pictures, little Christmas scenes for doors, peace doves for my bathroom, bunnies for my youngest granddaughter Kelia's nursery.

Jodie described, "In bright colors a 'Tree of Life' grows the height of one of the large hangings. It has the leaves of a black walnut tree at the base. Among the top branches is a white dove of peace, a blue bird of happiness, a cornucopia, spilling out apples, peaches, pears, prunes, cherries and an ear of corn. In the upper left, there is Pan, playing his music for the family blest with singers, composers, band leaders and other musicians. Below there is a beautiful symbolic horse representing those we've loved. Across from that a little red cocker spaniel represents Gretel and her descendants. There is a humming bird, sipping from a heavenly blue morning glory; a bumblebee, a dragonfly and

a butterfly. A big bunch of purple grapes with its leaves hangs from a branch of the tree. At the bottom there are red clover, lilies of the valley, wild roses and ivy, Mama's sweet violets; a thistle in bloom, goldenrod, foxglove, and lady slipper orchids. All of the things in the rug represented talents and interests of her family members."

Ethel's creativity knew no limit; her sense of beauty and color was ever alive and wonderful. She fit into this life as though she had been groomed for it. The inside of the house simply bloomed in her hands. She and Ed together often hunted for and found wonderful "old" things. She collected and decorated with copper and brass, used fine baskets, antique glass, unique pottery (some of which she made), besides her rugs and wall hangings, for decoration that didn't seem like decoration, but an integral part of the home. And there was her wonderful flower garden, stretching down the lane, out to the orchard, down in back as far as the hose would reach. The house was always filled with beautiful things from outside, whatever the season.

Lois, Edith's eldest daughter, told me that the family and all their friends saved worn-out garments for the rugs. Ethel often "reminded" us, or she would sometimes "wonder if we had a garment just the right color" for a certain rug. She also bought anything she could find at rummage sales, and of course later at Good Will. She had big baskets of colored rags all around her frame, like huge paint pots — orange, purple, several shades of blue and green and white, black and brown.   If she couldn't find a color she needed, she brought out the big kettles and had several batches being dyed on the stove.   The clotheslines were an amazing sight when hung with holey sweaters, brightly dyed wool long-johns, stockings, scarves, suits, and dresses.

Her rug-making went on always; the frame was never put away, and the baskets of braid or hooking strips, or uncut materials waiting to be used, sat beside it. She folded the edges of the strips under and basted them when she was braiding, so there were never any ragged edges showing. Then she laid the rug flat while she sewed the braids into the circle or oval — so perfect. Those rugs simply didn't wear out, and they never humped. Often she would hook the center part, and put braids around.   Whenever she was visiting with family or friends, she was cutting the strips or working on a new rug.

CHAPTER 6

The Wonderful Barn

The Farm had been the Caleb Davis place. According to Caleb's obituary, the original property was part of a donation land claim, over three hundred acres (probably 320, half a section). The fine barn was on the other side of the property line when the place was divided. On the east side of the barn was a big pen full of very large pigs. There were two black walnut trees and the pigs crunched the nuts up to eat.

Jodie tells about it: "When Dad bought the place, the half-section was split and the grand old barn was cut off our new section—it really stood on the other side of the lane. Dad opted to move it onto our property. I remember it well! Dad's brothers, Uncle Alf and Uncle Will Allworth, came down from Battle Ground, Washington, and with a crew, took down the barn, which had settled low enough that the men had to stoop a little to enter the door. They rebuilt it farther east on our side of the lane, using the same hand-made pegs and square nails and the hand-hewn beams, taking the old barn down piece by piece, numbering and charting each piece for perfect reassembly, and putting it back together, piece by piece, this time on proper concrete footings. It was now high and airy. I have a few of those old iron square nails in my jewelry box.

"The families came with the uncles, and the wives bustled about and prepared wonderful meals, which were spread on long plank tables for the men and their families. Children scrambled about—there were lots of children in the Allworth family. It was a real event, like something out of the pioneer stories. Everyone was having a wonderful time, and the barn was perfect. It had big lofts for the hay (and for the children to play in). The floor was dirt, except for a wood-plank floor on one side where there was a stable."

Jodie goes on, "Just behind the house was the stone fruit house which had been the ice house and root cellar, with thick sawdust-insulated walls for winter storage of root vegetables, squash, apples, and the hundreds of jars of fruit and meat and vegetables Mama canned. I remember the floor was falling through when we first saw it! Caleb Davis' name and the date of the home, 1878, are inscribed on a stone on the outside back wall.

"Ensconced under two big oaks was a wee tired-looking old house, nearly covered in moss, that I think surely would have been at one time a little home, maybe the first homestead. The trees looked as though they had been planted on either side of the path! There was even a small sun porch on one side. We later used this old house for a chicken house.

"A two-story implement shed sat across the barnyard from the barn, toward the house. Halfway back there was an open loft, with a stairway against the wall for access. All

manner of ancient horse-drawn farm equipment was in there, and also out in the grove and all around the place. Men came around to all the Farms buying up the metal junk, and we sometime later learned that most of it was shipped to Japan. Dad said it was probably used in the war against us. Clear, knot-free cedar lumber was used for the boards of the siding. One by one these mossy old buildings came down, and when the buildings were torn down, there were piles and piles of shingles to be stored for excellent kindling.

"The implement shed had to be removed to make way for the new milking barn—Dad had decided to have a dairy—which was then connected to the rebuilt hay barn. I remember the old smells of the milking area, where cows had been milked for so many years.

"The granary also had two floors. It sat between the house and the big barn, with the well house next to it. The granary was a square building with "stalls" to store grain, with a loading platform on the back with a sliding door. There was a good well—we always had enough water. The siding on all of these buildings (except the little old house) was put on vertically.

"Out back in the oak grove was a cement sheep dip pit, set into the ground. It was full of oak leaves, and I played in it. Later on the neighbors got together and actually used it to dip their sheep. It had a ramp down into the pit, and one coming out. The sheep were immersed in the middle, as the farmers ran them through one at a time. I don't recall how they got the water into it, but I do clearly recall the *smell* of the sheep dip!

"In the back yard of the main house was an outside privy. It was disposed of when the inside bathrooms were finished. I hated that because then I had to go clear into the house to the bathroom. I hid a gallon can upstairs in the implement shed and used that until I got caught!

"Under the grapevine-covered arbor, we later constructed the 'breezeway' leading to the house. Church pews from the little old church were put along the sides of the breezeway, for comfortable resting. A 55-gallon barrel sat at the corner to catch the rain from the gutters of the roof. I liked to watch the mosquito larvae squiggle around in it in summer, until Grampa poured oil in it. The oil made 'rainbows' on the surface of the water and killed the mosquitoes. The dust was still fairly deep around the house. I was always barefoot, and the dust didn't bother me any. After the sidewalks were poured, it was easier to put in lawns, but there remained lots of work smoothing, raking, seeding, and watering.

CHAPTER 7

Jodie Remembers

The dining room, next to the kitchen and east of the living room, was large enough for a great table that could easily seat twenty people, and sometimes did. Ethel's journal: "We bought nine dining room chairs at Edwards Furniture Store second hand department from Ade Sieberts who worked there, about 1925. Ed made fine needlepoint seat covers for them but over the years we wore them out so I hooked new covers." The table was large, and had several leaves, so that it could be extended. Nancy and Jodie tried to make a list of the people who had sat at that hospitable table, and found the numbers high: "Besides the six immediate family

members, were Grampa, Grandad Allworth, Bob Harvey,
Archie Carlon, Aunt Edith and her four girls, Lynne, Neil,
Jacki and Clark, Edward and Janet, Marlene, Kirby
Brumfield, Winston, Lea, Gay, Ralph, Peggy, Evelyn and
Norman and Lauri, the Wolfes, Sieberts, Stidds, Linden and
her family, the Samples, Windy and Mary, Dot and Otto—
the list goes on and on.

Most of the downstairs furniture was gathered over the
years, and was rich dark mahogany, lustrous cherry, fine-
grained walnut, or delicate rosewood. They scoured the
countryside and beyond for these lovely old pieces, which
the rural people were selling off, desperate to get some
money and when nothing else would sell. Fern Gibson, their
friend and knowledgeable antique dealer, always let them
know when there was something special she wanted them to
see. This search was fun and profitable and they soon
became very discerning, very selective.

All the windows were the old-fashioned tall narrow
ones, and they were early equipped with storm windows,
which had to be taken off or put on every spring and winter,
a big and tedious job. The windows were all washed before
the screens were put on for the summer. The curtains were
sheer lace, to the floor, and some of the rooms had draperies
of oatmeal-colored monks cloth. The 19th Century doorways
and windows of this house were not "standard," and the
very tall members of the family or guests bent their heads a
little while passing through the doorways. It was one of

those silly family jokes when
two of us would attempt to
go through the narrow door
together, and there would be
giggles as we pretended to be
stuck there.

Several doors led into the
kitchen—from the entrance
hall, from the dining room,
and from the laundry room.
After a few years, the south

end of the kitchen and the back porch were incorporated into a comfortable "keeping room," where the family usually gathered. The kitchen itself was large and open, with a hutch, an electric stove, replacing the old wood range, plus a wood-burning garbage burner, and a built-in dish cupboard with a glass front. All the storage was added on, as the old kitchens did not have built-in cabinets. The hutch, made especially for us by Will, was beautiful, with an enormous breadboard to pull out.

On every door and cupboard door and even inside the

cupboard doors, and on the wall space over the stove, Ethel painted a picture, sometimes a copy of an old master, or a little farm scene, or a lovely child. Once when I went out to the Farm, I found her on top of a step-ladder, painting delft blue and tan "tiles" on the ceiling, and they are there today.

Jodie knew the story of the bright red 19th century coffee mill at the end of the drainboard. "The antique coffee mill came from an old deserted homestead out Blodgett way. My husband and I were pasturing our Romney sheep up there one summer, and while tending the flock I saw a piece of a rusty metal wheel peeking up through the soil. A home had apparently rotted away or burned there (probably burned). Curious, I tugged at the wheel, finally getting a tree branch to dig more dirt off before the ground would give up—and wow! There were two wheels—and an old coffee grinder! I cleaned it up and took the prize to Mama and Dad. They had it cleaned, Mama painted it

bright red with period striping of cream color; Dad had a little wooden box drawer made to catch the ground coffee from the beans, and it was used for years."

Also in the kitchen was a rack of antique wooden kitchen tools, "purtles" from a bygone era hung on the wall. I remember that *purtles* was certainly a new word for me, and I added it with pleasure to my vocabulary, but I usually have to explain it when I use the word in conversation. It is so adequate to describe the variety of mixing spoons, turners, forks, tongs, and large collection of tools used in the kitchen. These were all wood, of course, and the rack was old polished maple, with large holes to hold the purtles!

Jodie remembers, "One of the changes was installing a swinging door between the kitchen and dining room. There were more than a few bumps and short words (and laughter) when two people were trying to go through from opposite sides. The telephone was on the wall on the kitchen side. While you were talking on the telephone, you might get bumped by someone coming through from the dining room side. It could also be especially touchy if one of the persons using the door was carrying a tray of food or a pitcher of milk or water."

Sumptuous meals emanated from that kitchen: home-made bread, thousands of big raisin-filled oatmeal cookies, great casseroles of chicken or turkey pies, delicate delicious divinity, even a little roast pig. Countless groups of Camp Fire Girls were brought to visit, and the girls always clustered close around Peggy while she told them loving stories about homemaking; little boys seemed awestruck at the wonder of such a place while they waited for the inevitable treat—warm cookies and cold milk or hot cocoa. Every child would go away bearing his own pencil with "Allworth Farm" imprinted upon it, and the memory of a "different, special place."

The front door was almost never used, and it always stuck a bit. Everyone except the occasional salesman came in through the breezeway. It actually startled us when anyone came to the front door, which the children called the "other door." We had to stop and think when the doorbell rang! There was a little gate in the fence, and a pretty brick path leading to the porch, but since most people drove rather than walked to the Farm, they came in from the large open play yard where they parked.

There was a brass bell with a lovely tone to ring at the outside back door opening into the entrance hall, which Ethel made into a little play school room for the children, with small old desks from a kindergarten or first grade classroom. She painted murals over the doors to the kitchen, living room, and a downstairs bedroom; added a hooked runner on the floor and a big copper jug, usually filled with bright leaves or flowers.

There was a perennial leak in the entry that baffled everyone who worked on it. So on rainy days, another fixture was a copper kettle to catch the drips. Even the new aluminum roof didn't solve the problem. I have no idea how many men—family and roofers—went up on that roof to find the spot where the water could come in. The leak was still there when the Corneliuses moved in!

The original house roof was also mossy, which worried all of us. Every time there would be a chimney fire—those chimneys were so tall—the roar was terrifying. It frightened everyone except Grandad Allworth, who couldn't hear it. The sparks would come out the top and land on the dry cedar shingles. Jodie says, "Mama was always nervous about it, and when I was little I would run as hard as I could down the road so I couldn't hear or see it. It would happen if there were too hot a fire or someone would throw in some loose papers that caught and floated up the chimney. Dad finally put on an aluminum roof—whew! We found a place around the chimney in Dad's attic closet where the wood was <u>charred</u> from the chimney burning out and getting so hot up there! We learned to be careful about the fires in the fireplaces at the Farm.

"There was a great winding wisteria vine that grew clear up the east side of the house and often had to be trimmed around the windows. I can see and smell it now as I write. When the bathroom windows were opened out in hot weather, it was so sweet on the shady side of the house. *(Sorry, now I weep with homesickness. This is my life and my only <u>home</u>. I don't remember ever missing the house in town. The Farm was always a great adventure for me.)*

"The memories come faster than I can write them down. I remember sitting in the tall grass out under the big oak, at the east end of the house, smelling the smells, hearing the sounds—bees droning, cows munching and lowing." Jodie had found her life. Jodie was always a free spirit, and here she had room to be totally herself, with horses, dogs, cats, cows, a haymow, neighbors, and a country school. When she started "remembering" for this book, she said: "I find I don't know where to end my descriptions. The memories keep coming, each one reminding me of something more. There was so much activity!

"When the work was being done on the porch, an old cistern was found, built from rocks and clay. Dad had it filled in for safety for the children.

"In my exciting memories, I can see the tree planting ceremonies—all the shrubs and trees arriving with their roots in big balls of soil wrapped with burlap; then the hole-digging, soaking, fertilizing, covering in and tamping down.

"Brick walks had to be reset to be level and even, fences straightened, wild myrtle pulled away and cut so the little picket fence could be painted fresh and white."

Nancy and Jodie were reminiscing together: "Mama also loved hammocks. Until the old Royal Anne cherry tree in the back yard died, we had a string hammock between it and the equally aged Bartlett pear tree. Without stays, it took concentration and skill to get into it without rolling over and out onto the ground with a bump. The neat thing was that you could lie down and draw it up around you, so theoretically, no one knew you were there. Never mind the round bump underneath where your bottom was. When the cherry tree died, Mama had a hammock hung between two big oaks at the south end of the play yard. We wore out one or two of those before she had one made of the staves from a wooden barrel. It was fun, but not nearly so versatile."

Jodie continues, "About 1937, we planted the forest, with all kinds of baby evergreens. They grew fast. Quail moved in. We really got upset when someone took a shot at our quail, and the shot hit the front of the house when Mama was working out in the yard! Owls also came to our forest, and pheasants—it became a wildlife resort. I loved to go down in there in the quiet shade when the trees got tall enough to be over my head. They are huge now, of course. The forest began early to have its own little ecosystem, with squirrels, chipmunks, raccoons, foxes, and birds. We would find tiny little mouse skeletons dropped by the owls. It was always fragrant, quiet. At night we could hear the unearthly calls of the owls, and sometimes we would see one."

Another "forest" came into being rather inadvertently, and later. Tony Van Vliet and his pretty wife Louise stayed in the apartment while he was going to school, and he planted a little Christmas tree farm next to the road, across from the forest below the west orchard after they smoothed the road curves. Not all the trees were sold from this enterprise, and today there is a lovely grove of large fir trees to complement the forest.

"Mama loved flag stones, and everywhere we went," Jodie remembers, "we hunted for and picked up flat stones to bring home. The stones did have a tendency to sink slowly out of sight, so we also had some pinkish cement walks poured, from the back door out to the play yard under the arbor, and out to the fruit house. I think it was brick past there. The cement was designed to look like flag stones, and broomed so it wouldn't be slick. Oh, and there were steps down from the laundry room and a little sidewalk to the clotheslines. Later a sidewalk outside the small laundry patio led to the lily pond by the two big oaks, where the old chicken house had been. That's where Dad put his beautiful begonia collection. The lavender hedge was east of the new sidewalk. A garden seat swing was added there, too. Out by the clotheslines, Dad had a huge clump of rhubarb.

"Most of Mama's many birdbaths were her own design. She had Harris Whitby pour cement bowls, first whole then later with a drain hole and cork so they would be easier to clean. Most were set on very rustic mortar and random rock pile/pillars or stumps in corners of the yard.

"Damson plum trees were planted near the rest of the orchard at the west end of the garden. They came from starts which had been brought across the plains by train with Great- Grandmother Sarah Waite Walker when she came out to live with Grampa, before he was married to our grandmother. Then new starts from those California trees were brought here from their Hanford, California home with the Walkers when they moved to Oregon. Now they were added to the orchard on the Farm. All of the members of the family have tried to have at least one of the trees, and Lea has several. They are prolific, and heavy bearers, and the jam is superb."

CHAPTER 8

Babies

Ethel reminisced happily, "Not too long after our move to the Farm, our Kent Sieberts was born, a beautiful baby boy. We then decided to have another child soon so they would be playmates. Edward and Jodie were six years apart, and Kent was more than six years after Jodie. So we had our Nancy Angenette just one year and six months after Kent, and they were perfect playmates. We called them 'the babies,' and they grew up on the Farm.

"I often bathed the two babies in the big double sink, easy and fun, both at once, and they loved it. When I was expecting Nancy I remember how hard it was going up and down stairs carrying our big baby boy, who wasn't walking yet, and I bulging with Nancy. When finally she was born, these were really busy times, but so dear. I had a large wicker baby buggy, and often took the babies for a ride down our country road for our outing. If the other children were at home, there would be one on a tricycle and one on a horse—we made quite a parade; of course, with a dog following along. When Grampa took <u>his</u> daily walk, the cats followed him—tails waving—cute. They loved him and 'helped' him while he whistled and worked in the garden.

"I used to sit on our big back porch in a huge rocking chair, a baby under each arm—so happy—rocking and singing, all three of us. Ed told me they could hear us clear out at the barn. I kept Nancy and Kent in a playpen on the back lawn where they could play and watch the dogs, especially our beautiful collie, Vee."

Part II:

GROWING UP

CHAPTER 9

Nancy & Kent

One of Nancy's earliest memories is of walking down our graveled lane, which had a hump in the middle. "I recall holding onto a hand above my head of a much taller person than I, who prevented me from slipping on the slope of that center hump. I wore toddler shoes with their slick leather soles. Mama told me my companion would have been Grampa, because he walked with me almost daily. My memories from those early times are spotty and vague, but I recall feeling generally at peace, and untroubled. I remember only a few of the household 'help'—from their pictures in the scrapbooks. My brother Edward, thirteen years older than I, lived in a separate world. Jodie had a set of activities and friends faintly recalled now.

"Kent was my friend and comrade. We played 'farms' behind the fireplace, with little rubber animals, fences built from Lincoln Logs, and trees of spools and green paper. We drew and cut out little animal fronts and backs and glued them to each end of a wooden spool, and colored them for realism. This way, we had as many animals as we wanted. We made trees by fringing and rolling up green tissue paper and poking the rolled end into a spool.

"When World War II started, Kent painted the inside of one lower bookshelf to be the ocean, and set up his collection of small lead ships. He had them all—battleships, destroyers, aircraft carriers, submarines. The little farm games ended, and Kent had the bottom shelves by the fireplace for his war games. He had tiny lead soldiers, and he made battle and war scenes.

"The dairy kept us all very busy. I recall walking to the fields to bring in the cows for milking. High rubber boots protected me from the deep muck, but often were held by the sucking wet stuff and my foot slipped out, and I would have to clutch the fence. I learned pretty quickly to stay near the fences. The cows <u>knew</u> they were to come, but perversely waited until I came to get them, and then they passed me and took themselves to the warm barn for grain and hay, and cleaning. When I was small, still too young to do much else, Kent and I were assigned to washing udders, feeding grain to the cows, and of course shoveling the fresh 'pies' away from the milking area.

"Along the roadways, in the vineyard and at the edges of the oak woods, there were huge thickets of blackberry brambles. Most of the berries were Himalayas, but there were also Evergreens. If we timed it right, we could pick many gallons of the luscious Himalayas, and if we were careful, we could do it without major damage from the sharp thorns. Mama canned them, made juice, jam, pies, cobblers, and of course we ate them raw and on cereal. The Evergreens were good, but had very large seeds, were not so juicy as the Himalayas, and the thorns were wicked. Usually, we didn't bother with them if we could get the Himalayas as they were better, anyway.

"We also had to fight thistles, which often grew in and around the brambles. You had to really want those berries! A given in Western Oregon when harvesting wild things was to keep a sharp eye out for the characteristic three-part leaves of the poison oak bushes.

"I'd been told that bears had been seen in the woods around the place, but I never saw one. There were lots of deer, and frequently we did see those, especially across the road on the Alnutt place.

"There were summer evenings when all of us kids [Edward, Jody, Kent, and Nancy] would play hide and seek around the big oak yard and front yard. I remember it seemed a little spooky, because the sea breeze was nearly

always blowing at dusk, and the shrubs and trees swayed and whispered, making constantly changing shadows and many little sounds. The games were a prickly kind of fun. There may have been others who played with us — I don't remember. I was at the age that the only reason I could be out running about late was that Edward was there, and I wasn't accustomed to being outside after dark.

"First Edward, and then Kent, often worked at putting together the painfully complex model airplanes of balsa wood and tissue paper. They were very impressive when completed, and took many, many hours to construct. This seemed much more of an achievement than gluing together pre-formed pieces of plastic that are available today."

CHAPTER 10

The Dairy

Jodie loves to tell, "To begin his herd for the dairy, Dad bought five big Holstein heifers. But— *I'll never forget!* — those big long-legged critters <u>ran</u> — I think they went over every fence in the county! They never slowed down. I remember Dad being really mad. I can't say if we ever got them back on the place or if he sold them 'as is,' or if he ever even had to pay for them. He switched to little soft, doe-eyed Jerseys for his dairy. I have pictures of those cows, and I can name them now.

"Aunt Edith came to the Farm several times during her life, and the time I remember most is when we had the dairy, and she brought two or three cows. I don't remember much about the others, because she and Dad talked it over and decided that only one could stay. She chose to keep an old dark gray tinged-with-black cow named *Delphinium*, who definitely had a mind of her own. Among other unique features, her udder hung so low that her teats touched the ground, and in order to milk her, Dad had to have a platform built for her to lift her rear end so the milking machine could be used. She even had scratches and cuts from stepping on them as she walked." Jodie and Nancy believe that *Delphinium* was acually part of the herd for some years, until after the fire.

Even though she was small, Jodie recalls, "The first year the whole family helped plant kale one plant at a time by hand for the cows, all down from the front of the house toward the road, where the forest is now. Cousin John

Halvorson was staying with us then and helping. Everything had to be done by hand, and we all laboriously carried great buckets of water to keep the kale moist. Maybe we didn't even have hoses then, or they didn't reach that far. I think we didn't plant kale more than that one year, as we had other feed for them after that. The area was used for part of the orchard later.

"Our fields were plowed, dised, raked, rolled, harrowed and planted using a team of horses which came with the Farm. There were Nell and Nellie, sisters; and Molly, an old chestnut. I liked to follow in the furrow as Gene Dengue walked behind the horses with the lines over his shoulders, plowing. I thought it was fun to watch the fat worms get uncovered and wriggle back into the dirt. I can hear the grunting of the horses as they strained at their tugs and dug in with all four feet to pull the plows, or the hay wagons topped high and groaning up the hill lane to the barn. Sweat dripped and lather slithered from under the harness on the

horses, while the chains on the end of the tugs (or *traces* as Dad called them) jingled, mingling with the slap of the leather along their sides. And I can still hear Dad calling the cows!"

Ethel's journal: "We asked my Dad to make out a list of trees to plant for our orchard. He was in seventh heaven, selecting the trees and planning the arrangement. He knew so much about fruit, and laid out a wonderful orchard." There were red delicious, winesap, Jonathan, gravenstein, Mac-Intosh, yellow banana, yellow transparent and Spitzenburg apples; then quinces, winter pears, Bartlett pears, plums, prunes, cherries (Bing, yellow Royal Annes, Black Republicans, and sour pie).

South of the orchard was an open place, about half an acre, so a big vegetable garden was put in. Still farther south of that many berry vines — loganberries, blackberries, raspberries, gooseberries, grapes and currants, were planted. At the west end of the open place were beehives, next to the fence by the oak grove.

Jodie remembers Grampa taking care of the goats, and dusting the garden for bugs with cheesecloth bags of ashes from the wood furnace and fireplaces. He worked hard hoeing, raking, and spading in the garden. He loved to garden, had always been an excellent gardener, and he whistled softly as he worked. He kept the shop meticulously neat, with the tools hanging, clean and shiny and ready to use, little drawers of supplies, caches of nails, screws of all sizes and styles.

CHAPTER 11

Grampa Walker

My Dad was in his late seventies, a sturdy, charming man, intellectual and studious, who had been in teaching and administration for most of his life. He was completely satisfied to have a hand in this family project, and lived on the Farm the rest of his life.

We had moved to Portland to live with the Allworths when I was ten. Ethel once told me that our father was one of her best friends. They had many years of companionship when the rest of the family was away. One of his delightful characteristics was that he "never knew a stranger." He made everyone welcome, and when Ethel was busy, he would graciously visit with the guests, with warm hospitality. He was a sparkling conversationalist, and seemed to have an endless fund of historical knowledge of the Western world.

Our young mother had died when I was small, and he never ceased to miss her. Sometimes, as he prepared for bed, he could be heard talking quietly to her, "Effie, this has been a busy day." He loved to be with the family, and the Farm was ideal for him. He was warm, comfortable, cared for, and had his many dear ones around him. He had a certain amount of authority, simply by virtue of his intelligence and good judgment, and being there made it possible for him to live well. He had lost his savings in the 1929 crash, so actually had very little money of his own—this was before the days of Social Security—there had been no "safety net" in those dark days. I never knew this, when I was growing up—we certainly did not seem impecunious! I always earned my own living after I was eighteen, but he bought my school books, my typewriter, shoes and other necessities until then, and Dot or Ethel made my pretty clothes.

He was completely at home in his little room, and in this loving home. He always helped Ethel, bringing wood for the fires, mending things that needed to be fixed, creating useful tools where there didn't seem to be one that worked. He tried to never be a care or a bother. If he and Ed disagreed about anything, he would be quiet and non-confrontational.

CHAPTER 12

Upstairs

From Jodie's memories: "I loved my room, a corner room upstairs. I had to go through the folks' bedroom to reach it. Located over what had become the music room behind the fireplace, it had two tall windows looking west and north. My favorite window faced north down the hill  toward the road, where the little bridge crossed over the slough. In the summertime I could hear thousands of frogs singing from there. I remember lying on sheets on the floor to sleep in the heat of summer. Both windows would be open. Dad had a wardrobe built for me to hang clothes in, and two great big drawers at the bottom where my things could be put away. They let me paper one wall solid with horse pictures, and on that same side of the room was my dollhouse.

"I had a <u>wonderful</u> dollhouse, made from apple boxes. These were wooden bushel boxes that are not made any more. Grampa carved little beds and chairs, and Mama wallpapered the rooms from cut-out pictures. It had an upstairs, kitchen, bedrooms, bathroom, and much more, thanks to Mama's ingenuity. You could see scenes out of the windows; there were tiny braided rugs out of bright yarn, or paper rugs cut out of the Montgomery Ward catalogs,

minute pictures hanging on the walls also from magazines. It was so perfect — I think it finally had at least nine rooms.

"I used to sing my Western songs out of the window at the top of my voice into the night — I liked to hear my own voice carrying down toward the bridge. *(I have always missed the love and security of my room.)*

"Edward's big room at the head of the stairway was directly over the dining room. He also had a window toward the road, and one facing the balcony, and best of all, one at the back toward the river, where you had a view of the fields and woods. Nancy reminded me that on a clear day you could see Mt. Jefferson, the Three Sisters, and other peaks of the Cascade Mountain Range. I think that Dad must have put in the row of small square windows like the ones in the bathroom, and there were window seats built all along under the windows, with lift lids for storage.

"I loved to sit on the window seat and gaze off into the mystical distance toward the river. It was so beautiful. Like the bathroom windows, these were framed on the outside by the wisteria that covered the back of the house.

"Edward as a child loved to send for things, and once sent away for and received a baby alligator. Mama liked to tell about it. The little creature was about 18 inches long, and lived in a tub in Edward's room. Finally, it calmed down and they assumed it went into hibernation. Thinking it was not warm enough, Edward placed the alligator on the radiator in his room—and waited, and waited, and waited. After some weeks, he and Mama decided to check it out, and found it completely stiff and dry. It must have been dead for quite a long time.

"He had little live traps he made, and caught chipmunks that way. We had a maid we called 'Big Elizabeth' (in contrast to 'Little Elizabeth' who had worked for us previously). Big Elizabeth was cleaning in Edward's room. When she started to make his bed, she was confronted by an angry chattering chipmunk that had been sleeping under the covers. After that, Elizabeth refused to make his bed!

"There was an accumulation of 'treasures' in the window seat that all the children loved to explore. I remember the tiny pretty blown glass objects Edward had on his dresser, sitting on a mirror.

"Mama and Dad's room was large. When the barn was moved, and Uncle Will logged the black walnut trees from the ex-pig pen, he made many things from the fine wood, including a great bedstead. It was a four-poster for the master bedroom, extra long to accommodate Dad's height and stiff leg. Uncle Will also made two study tables, cutting boards for everyone, and he paneled his own office and built his big desk."

This was before the era of king-sized beds and linens. Ethel cut up sheets and sewed them onto the ends and sides of double-bed sheets to make them large enough, and they had to have the box springs and mattress especially made. She always said that she occupied the northwest corner of that huge bed, and let Ed have the rest. Jodie said that her mother used a little stepstool to climb into bed. I have often thought what a chore it must have been for her to make that bed alone. I know that for many years they made it up together. She moved into the pretty youth bed when she was alone in later years.

The children were not allowed out on the balcony on the outside of the master bedroom. Ed had a strong trellis built from the ground up to the balcony to be used for a fire escape. Jodie tattles, "Nancy was naughty once and climbed down the fire escape from the little attic room, but that was strictly forbidden, too." Lauri and Lea have confessed to me that they did climb down the trellis, <u>very carefully</u>, and certainly daringly; punishment for such a violation would have been swift and drastic. An exquisite blue clematis grew on the front trellis, and on national holidays the flag flew proudly and high from the balcony. It was always there every day of WWII.

Jodie's description: "The master bedroom had four doors, one to my bedroom, one to the attic, one to the balcony, and one to the stairs, so there was a good deal of traffic through there, even at night sometimes. There were

two small high windows, and one tall one. Later on Mama put a lovely antique sleigh bed where the crib was when the babies were small. The other furnishings were three good-sized dressers, a small, flax spinning wheel, and a little folding rocking chair that had come over the plains in a covered wagon." Mrs. Briggs, a neighbor on South 13th Street, gave it to her, and Peggy covered it with a piece of antique carpeting. The beautiful cedar chest — which was Peggy's "hope chest" — fit at the foot of the bed. She hung the walls with her hooked rugs, Ed's framed medals, pictures of the children and quaint mottoes; the floors were polished and adorned with the hooked and braided rugs. It was spacious and gracious.

CHAPTER 13

Attic Room

Over the furnace room was an attic room just off the master bedroom, beyond a long walk-through closet. There was one small window in the south wall. The chimney from the furnace came up through there just inside the door that opened to the closet, keeping the room warm. Kent and Nancy bunked in this little attic room when they left their cribs, and Jodie remembers being banished there "when I had measles and mumps. I also played dolls there. My *Rosebud* had a bed, and Mama's beautiful gentle-faced Victorian *Cordelia*, too. There were exquisite clothes for the dolls, made from scraps of velvet, silks and brocades. The doll beds had sewing thread spools for legs, and they had pillows and sheets and coverlets, all fashioned by the same loving hands."

Before the walls were finished, trunks and boxes were stored in the corners under the eaves containing marvelous hats and dresses and little pointed button-up shoes from long ago, never played with as "dress-ups," but looked at with awe and admiration by all the little girls. Also in a corner was "Peachtree," Ethel's dress form she made in her Home Economics class in college — she had studied to be a teacher. We all loved "Peachtree," made to her own slim proportions, a quaint token of the days when ladies made or had made

all their own clothes,which they often did without patterns. "Peachtree" was often draped tastefully with elegant shawls and jewelry.

Later this room was turned into a tiny bedroom, with a cot at each side, painted walls and a real ceiling, and it was warmer. There was a marvelous collection of very old comics, stacks of them, a treasure for all the kids. In the 1960s when I would visit from Gilchrist, I would often bring my dear friend Connie Sample, and her two children, Beverly and James. Jim would arrive with his eyes shining, say a polite and almost reverent hello to Ethel, whom he called "Mrs. Worth," and make a beeline for that attic, and we might not see him for hours.

Nancy describes the little room as "cozy, but it was also a scary place to me when Kent and I were occupying it. The chimney from the furnace reached up through the closet that was to the right as you entered the attic, and sometimes it was quite hot to the touch. I was afraid a fire might separate us from the rest of the family, so I used to hurry by it and not look. I liked it better when the door of the walk-through closet was open against the chimney, covering the closet spaces behind it. Lots of things were stored in the cupboards behind the two army cots Kent and I slept on. Squirrels used to get into those cupboards, and we could hear them rolling their nuts and acorns around in the walls, rattling around as though they were playing a tiny game of bowling. The worst thing of all was the occasional bat or two that would get in through one of the open windows. The whirring sound they made was like nothing else, and it terrified me. I remember Dad swatting at them with a fly swatter!"

There was always an unsettled little bone of contention between Ed and Peggy concerning the windows—for Peggy, like the rest of the Walker family, they had to be open all year long, and before they had the screens made, little flying creatures had easy access.

One of the upstairs bedrooms was made into a spacious bathroom, looking toward the East, down over the pastures to the river. This pastoral view was shared by the dining room, kitchen, and Edward's bedroom. At no time in that informal family was there any privacy in that bathroom. That's just the way it was. It was decorated like the rest of the house with Ethel's paintings and rugs. This bathroom was used by everyone in the family, sometimes all at once. The *piece de resistance* was the funny pair of large feet, hooked in soft pink wool, placed appropriately in front of the toilet.

The bathtub was old-style, standing alone, with a permanent gold-orange-colored ring caused by the iron in the water, which Ethel referred to as the 'jewels in our bath.' Through all the years she scrubbed at that ring. Nancy once said to her mother that she would probably never have a date, because she was sure she smelled mostly of Clorox! There was no shower. It just was a very special, very unusual, and much-admired bathroom! I wish mine were half as large! But I'll confess, you had to get used to having lots of company.

A tiny bathroom with a shower was added downstairs and a bedroom for Grampa Walker.

CHAPTER 14

Downstairs

In the west end of the living room there was a piano, a little pump organ which traveled to the yard for weddings, and stacks of sheet music and music lesson books for children. Our Dad had given our mother the little ebony Emerson upright piano for an engagement present. It had real ivory keys; most of them have now been replaced — not with ivory, of course — as they have become worn and chipped. Every child in the family learned to play on that piano.

There were footstools and big and small chairs, a fine old roll-top desk, and on the hearth a tub of walnuts or filberts with a nutcracker handy.

The beautiful antique upright grand piano that was bought for Nancy, and that she has now, came much later. Nancy tells: "The Bouden piano, sometimes referred to in our family as the 'rosewood piano,' came to the Farm in the 1950s, while I was in college. It was custom-made in Germany by the Ronisch Company, fashioned of several quality woods and stained to look like rosewood. There were two pairs of sterling silver candlesticks to provide light, and a sterling silver handle at each end, presumably so the piano could be lifted by them. It was much too heavy for that of course, so the handles remain just for decoration.

"The piano was a wedding gift to a beloved daughter, who with her new husband, emigrated to the United States around 1850, before the Panama Canal. It sailed around the

horn of South America on a clipper ship to get to the West Coast. The Boudens had one daughter, who was a talented music teacher of many instruments, but who never married. Miss Bouden, who had been my brother Edward's guitar teacher, lived to her 90s. The beautiful, ornate piano was purchased for me from her estate, since she had no heirs who were interested in it."

Standing by the staircase was the tall grandfather clock, two hundred years old with all wooden operating parts, a loud tick that could be heard all over the house, and a bonging chime on the hour that took some getting used to. They found it some place in Central or Eastern Oregon, and paid $125 for it! It kept meticulous time. Our Dad used to sing a hearty song about the grandfather clock that kept perfect time, but "it stopped, never to go again, when the old man died." He knew all the old songs — that was fun.

Hanging on the wall was the treasured inheritance of a magnificent "wedding ring shawl." It had come from Mrs. Millard Fillmore, the President's wife, who was a cousin of Grandmother Bagley [Mama's mother]. Our Dad would never let us tell anyone of that distant relationship, because he had such a poor opinion of President Fillmore. He was such a loyal Republican it was difficult for him to believe there were any good Democrat presidents! The shawl was huge, and yet it was so fine that it could be drawn through a wedding ring, according to tradition.

Also in the living room, against an unused door that led into the downstairs bedroom, was the elegant tall secretary. This was their first antique piece, and they bought it from

Fern. They paid $27 for it. On the
mantel over the fireplace, they placed
the carved Philippine bookends we
had sent home. Several fine lamps
shed direct light for readers, and
added to the *decor* with their fancy
shades, one a Tiffany. There was a
green table where the grandfathers
played their games of cribbage, and
two small tables Neil had made with
stunning tops of Eastern Oregon
thunder-egg slices, inlaid in beautiful
patterns and designs.

"In the evenings we often read
aloud as a family, each one a
chapter," Jodie goes on. "We read
classics like *Ivanhoe, Knights of the
Round Table, Little Women,* and many other 'good books.'
Dad would be working his needlepoint for the chairs in the
dining room. He had learned to do this during his long stay
in the army hospital after WWI. He had also made beautiful
yarn rugs and pretty trays. Mama darned socks, and cut rug
rags. Their hands seemed always busy."

The richness of this house opened its arms to all. Three
fireplaces glowed warmth in the winter; high ceilings and
surrounding trees kept it cool and sweet in the heat of
summer. Jodie and Nancy and I, and probably Lois and her
sisters, also remember that it was a huge job to keep it up and
shiny. The carvings on the antique furniture had to be
dusted frequently and carefully; the floors, being old wood,
must always be polished; the many rugs on the floors were
vacuumed carefully. Among us all, we always had it "ready
for company," and were proud of it.

In late years, the keeping room became a little crowded,
with the large television set, Ed's big chair and footrest, and
the huge old desk; and a cot covered with bright cushions.
But it was cozy. Ethel put a gorgeous brass tray on the
elegantly carved wood mantel, and the grandmother clock,

like the grandfather clock in the living room, two hundred years old and still keeping perfect time. It was not noisy like the grandfather clock. At all seasons, there would be one of Ethel's exquisite arrangements in a stunning vase. An old copper bedwarmer with a long carved handle was suspended from the mantel, and all of the fireplace tools were antiques.

At Christmas time, there would be a Madonna and child, or children playing in the snow, or some other beautiful scene, covering the big window. They were for some years created by Nancy, and kept to use again.

A new laundry room was built off the kitchen, with a small bedroom above. The back door opened from it to the clothesline area — past the fragrant lavender patch. A patio was laid right next to it, with a rock fireplace, which always smoked. A rock wall defined the area. A large seedling black walnut tree grew there until it began to be a nuisance, then it was removed and the wood used, some of it by John Adair.

Nancy tells: "Some years later, Mama wanted to have a spinning wheel made for me to use with the mohair from my goats. We spoke with John Adair, our neighbor at the Farm, and he apologized that he had no more cherry wood — all he had was the large stump from the black walnut tree that had been removed from the corner of the laundry room at the Farm that was an unexpected thrill — so the spinning wheel was crafted from that symbolic hunk of wood, and equipped with all hand-made brass fittings — a truly lovely piece of furniture that performs perfectly."

Jodie remembers that Ed had a small house built for Gene Dengue, the helper, and his family. She says it was very small, but "four times bigger than what they had been living in. It was out in a clear spot at the end of the stump patch. Mama fed the little children, and made them clothes."

A double garage was built (not double by today's standards). Eventually, an apartment was added above it. At different times, different people lived up there, including Edith and her girls, several young college families, and Norman and me (for a few months after the war).

CHAPTER 15

Parents

Vivid in Jodie's memories of her youth: "Discipline was a way of life at the Farm, and economy was a necessity. The grandparents didn't have Social Security income, of course. I had what I thought were darling dresses made from colorful feed sacks (pretty prints not made any more) in grade school."

Nancy enlarges on this: "For several years, grain for the cows could be found in beautiful flower-printed fabric grain bags, for only a few cents extra. The fabric from these feed sacks was a muslin weight and weave, and Mama and I made blouses, skirts, dresses, and jumpers from them. Often Dad took me along so I could pick out the prints I wanted from those available. There were some that were, in my opinion, less attractive. After the grain was dumped into the big wooden bins at the barn, we took the sacks and picked out the seams, washed and ironed the cloth, and then cut and sewed it into garments. Flour sacks, a much finer fabric, also came in bright and lovely prints."

Jodie adds: "The pennies were stretched sometimes painfully, in the beginning, but we always had more than plenty to eat. We all carried our lunches, every day. We ate lots of root vegetables and greens, always served in delicious ways. For breakfast we had cereal, toast, and fruit. In later years we also had bacon and eggs, but in those earlier, leaner years, we were satisfied with goldenrod eggs on toast, and a half slice of bacon each for Sunday morning breakfast—and I became addicted to bacon on that half slice! We had hot biscuits often, with home-made butter. Milk and cottage cheese were staples in our diet. Dad and Aunt Edith especially liked the thick Jersey cream that you could spoon out—it was almost the consistency of ice cream."

Peggy Allworth's Goldenrod Eggs on Toast

> *6 hard-boiled eggs*
> *4 tablespoons butter*
> *4 tablespoons flour*
> *2 cups whole milk or light cream*
> *Salt*
> *Toast slices*

> *Cook eggs until firm. Leave in hot water and peel one at a time. Just before peeling, hold egg in cold running water or in a bowl of cold or ice water. Shell will peel very easily.*

> *Make white sauce by blending butter and flour and adding milk. Cook until thick in top of double boiler. Chop egg whites and fold into white sauce. Put egg yolks through coarse sieve.*

> *Cut round pieces from center of toast slices. Cover with creamed egg sauce and top with sieved golden yolks. (Toast crusts may be saved for bread puddings, dressings, or crumbs.)*

Jodie continues: "Both of our parents were strict task masters. Though I think perhaps the boys had the most difficult or strenuous jobs, we <u>all</u> worked very hard, and there was little praise. It was just expected. There was also not much demonstrative affection. It wasn't austere by any means, but communication was not so well understood in those days, and we were not asked for our opinion very often. Our parents just assumed that we knew they loved us, and they felt it was not necessary to talk about it. Punishment could be fairly harsh, and swift, so we were generally obedient, if not always willingly so.

"Nancy had more of the 'family quality' time as she was growing up, because she stayed at home through college. She learned how to make her own clothes by the time she was fourteen."

CHAPTER 16

Guests

The men of the family would sometimes gather in the space behind the fireplace to listen to boxing matches and college games that were out of town, when they couldn't go to them. Ed had lifetime passes to all the college sports because of his championship wrestling and football at OAC. When the college had home games, the old college chums would come to attend, and stay over, and they <u>always</u> came for Homecoming. Those were great parties. There was never any drinking at the Farm, but the merriment was supreme. The Sieberts, Browns, and Stidds from Portland, and other college friends from far and wide, seldom missed.

The weather could be pretty bad, but everyone braved the elements, went to the games, came back to the Farm for warmth and food and music and laughter and fun. One time Peggy and I were snuggled in our blanket on the bleachers

rooting for our team, when we heard the woman in front of us refuse the peanut vendor with the blunt and very audible statement, "Oh no! I never eat peanuts. They tie me up tighter than a drum!" We quietly and secretly giggled through the rest of the game.

I remember when Norman and Ade Sieberts were standing in the kitchen, having a cup of hot coffee, replaying the afternoon football game with gusto, when Ade gestured excitedly, sending Norman's cup flying across the kitchen. I laughed until I hurt, not only at seeing the cup take flight, but at their stunned expressions. Ade was funny, anyway.   We loved the Sieberts.

CHAPTER **17**

Work in Progress

Fields and orchards, gardens and forests were planted—
the whole place was always a "work in progress." Jodie
tells of those beginning days, "Before the barn was moved, I
was given a choice of whether I wanted to work in the house
or the barn—I chose the barn! My Bubby (Edward) was
there, and there was always something happening there! I
think now as I look back that sometimes when I was out by
myself in the grove or the barn or tall grass, maybe I was
hiding from the bustle and <u>endless</u> errands and tasks that
involved everyone. That's what it took, of course. There are
a few pictures of the Farm as it was when we moved, with
the front yard and the house looking so <u>bare</u>, and the back
yard overgrown.

"I learned how to use a manure shovel and how to
measure and feed grain, and to herd cows. It was usually
Edward's and my job to go down and hunt for the cows with
new calves so we could bring the newborn calves up to
safety. There were no dog packs then to be wary of, because
no one could afford to have more than one big dog to feed;
many households had none. But the big circles of menacing
buzzards over the birthing cows prompted us to hustle so
the babies wouldn't be attacked before they could stand.
Even then, Dad wouldn't let us shoot the buzzards, because
'they had their job to do in the scheme of things.' They
certainly always took care of the afterbirth!

"When summertime became really hot, there would be
circles of them spiraling in the skies over the land, searching

for death for a meal. Once I found a newborn calf which couldn't defend itself encircled on the ground—big buzzards were standing around it with their ugly beady eyes, waiting. I had to chase them away. There were several, and they seemed to be extremely hungry and greedy, and the heifer which had calved was afraid of them. I had to carry the tiny calf clear up to the barn even before it was dried off, then had to go back after the heifer, who was sure the buzzards had her baby.

"Along in November and December, thousands upon thousands of Canada geese would stop to rest down near the river—they would come and go in great flocks, or settle down and stay awhile. We could hear their chattering up at the house. In the fields there were China pheasants and little California quail. Down away from the house, along the drainage ditch and to the river, you'd often come onto a Great Blue Heron, standing on one leg among the cattails, contemplating the slough waters, immobile as a statue, as though he were posing for a picture.

"Near the river there was a circle of trees around a very small field which always flooded over in the winter. When the waters receded it left a hidden slough along the trees. I was quite young and trudging along lost in my make-believe thoughts down there one day when I startled a heron. Of course he startled me in return, rising out of the water right in front of me. I had never seen such a great bird with that enormous wingspread. I thought it was a stork going to take me away! I ran home as fast as I could go, and of course he flew the other way. Later on, I approached the area with greater caution and peeked through the brush, and did see one now and then.

"I really thought in those days that it rained nine months out of the year. Of course the flowers and trees and grass were luxurious and so green. Mama loved it—the coolness, the mists, the fog. Must have been our British blood (*a long way back, honey—we've been here since before the Revolution!*). She could not handle much heat, and always seemed to be much too warm.

"Winding through the fields from clear up at the house was a drainage ditch that came from the spring over on the Alnutt place. It was almost dry in the late summer, except for some small marshy pools where frogs and polliwogs remained. Edward and I explored along the ditch. Down past the second field, it was lined with overhanging willows (lots of pussy willows) and balsam and wild flowers.

"I loved it when Mama would make cute pictures with the pussy willows stuck on paper, and draw little whiskers  on their tiny faces, and little tails, and had them sitting on fences. Mama practiced drawing characters like stick people, and told me one time she would like to draw cartoons. I have found quite a few of her practice sheets.

"The ditch would come alive with beautiful multi-colored dragonflies, who were after the mosquitoes. Honey bees droned in the wild flowers. In the last big field before the river, there were tall balsam trees, and their sweet fragrance lent itself to an idyllic scene and time. When I smell a balsam tree, it takes me right back there with a wave of homesickness.

"Spring and summertime down at the river, warm, sunny, quiet, peaceful—meant butterflies, birds, wild flowers, and all kinds of water grasses—cattails, where rivulets lingered along the edges of the stream—I liked to climb down the sandy bank of the river and twiddle my toes in the water. All of the big kids swam, but I was so afraid of the water.

"There was a mossy old tree leaning out over the water and we pulled the licorice plants (ferns) off it and chewed on the roots. There were beautiful lush trilliums, little yellow Johnny-jump-ups, hundreds of buttercups and bachelor buttons. I loved them all, but the pretty wild columbines

were fun because we'd nip off the little points in the back and suck out the pretend honey.

"There were all of the native birds—robins, swallows, towhees, juncos, finches, chickadees, sparrows, hummingbirds, blackbirds, meadowlarks, and migrating visitors like Baltimore Orioles and cedar waxwings. In the fields, we had crows, and besides the buzzards, geese and ducks, and China pheasants, there were always grouse, quail, and bobwhites.

"In the garden were little green snakes, and the bigger brown snakes that ate mice. Because we had lots of mice, we had all kinds of owls, and hawks. There were plenty of yellow jackets, black hornets, honeybees and bumblebees. I was always barefooted, so had my share of stings and swollen toes, as well as stubbed ones!

"My cousins Delores, Ann, Celia and Lois lived with us at the farm for a time while they were all in school. Delores was my best chum for years. We used to dress up and put on 'plays' in the old 'chicken house' so Mama dressed up Dad, Kent and Nancy to come to our 'play.' We were very impressionable and when they took us to a circus, we started riding QP and Dolly standing like 'Roman riding'."

CHAPTER 18

Water

Mary's River meandered all through that area, and passed along the bottom of the Farm," tells Jodie. "It was 'far away' — when I was little, it seemed a very long way to walk. There were areas of thick scrub oak and underbrush. Edward found Indian arrowheads, chipped from obsidian, and some looked as though they were made from a type of agate. Calapooyans, our 'local tribe,' were basically farming and fishing people. They had lived along the banks long before our time. The spirits of those Indians who once camped and fished there might be close, I thought. The tiniest arrowheads were probably for fishing and hunting small game.

"I found a wooden pack-saddle in the brush, a <u>treasured</u> find. Mama painted it and we still have it in the family, sixty years later.

"In the wintertime, when Mary's River would overflow its banks, and it seemed as though the rain pelting down would never cease, the whole river bottom lands would be black with the Canada geese on their great migration. Maybe that's part of the reason the soils on river bottom lands are so rich. Sometimes Edward would 'pop' a goose or two and Mama would fix one for dinner.

"I used to love to ride QP down along next to the irrigation ditch and watch the water fly from out her hooves. She loved it, too. Once, though, we zigged when we should have zagged, and I went right in, and both of us went under. We got too close to the edge, the ditch turned and we didn't. All I could see was a solid sheet of water—and we were about halfway down to the river itself. We did manage to scramble out, soaked and bedraggled, and galloped home. Pure fun, and just scary enough to be exciting for both of us!

"There was always lots of standing water in the wintertime from run-off and from the spring over on the Alnutt place. In the heavy rainy season the water backed up into a large pond there before running over the road onto the Ingles' place where it cut through, then onto our place. Edward and I used to 'ice skate' in our shoes on that pond when it froze hard enough. When the County put a culvert under the road, and cleaned out the brush, the water didn't back up quite so much. John Adair and his wife bought the corner of the land just below our line, next to our lane, and turned that wet corner into a marvelous grouping of ponds for wild waterfowl. They were dear friends and neighbors, and through the years their place was a pleasure to see. This path of water then wound its way the length of our place clear to the river.

"Once while Ned Sieberts was visiting, Edward and Ned built a cabin down at the bottom of the Farm. They made wooden bunk beds, and stayed there sometimes. I, of course, wasn't allowed, but after they had later abandoned it, I fixed little paths to and from the door, edged with rocks, and transplanted wild flowers among them, and played happily there."

"There were two or three spots that made really nifty swimming holes," Nancy remembers. "There was one just south and east of the big bridge down past the Rycraft place—it may have been on their place. We used to go there on hot days sometimes and splash around, play, and swim--that was where I first learned to swim. I remember both Edward and Jodie being there, and some of their friends.

You had to ignore the water bugs, minnows and salamanders (water dogs) that lived there. It was a big disappointment when it was declared off limits because a dead calf was found upriver, and the river was too contaminated for swimming. My own favorite pastime at any part of the river was looking for wildflowers and watching the beautiful ducks, especially the lovely little wood ducks, feeding or fixing their nests.

"There were always friends — little friends and big friends, old and young, new and lasting ones. They came, and they brought their friends. They sometimes stayed awhile, or just for juice and cookies, or for one of Mama's gracious, bounteous meals.

"Aunt Edith and Mama made bread, and the best treat came when the hot loaves first came out of the oven, and Mama let us slice off a steaming hunk and put fresh butter on it. Home-made bread was awkward for school lunch sandwiches, because it didn't hold together very well, but the flavor was wonderful."

"In our dairy at that time we had Jersey cows, which gave milk with a high percentage of cream. Dad separated out extra cream so the milk was worth more from the buyer. Mama found a couple of old Daisy butter churns, square glass jars — probably gallon-size, with tops equipped with gears, a handle to turn, and wooden paddles that reached down into the jars. She would put the cream into the churn,

and one of us would turn the handle steadily, not too fast, until we made butter. The folks found several old wooden butter molds, and Mama pressed the fresh butter into them, after she had salted it, of course. We had round butters that had flowers or leaves and other decorations in relief on the tops. Usually she froze the extra pats to preserve them, but even then sometimes they became rancid if we didn't use them soon enough.

"During the summer, with all of the many folks at the Farm living, working, visiting, and eating, we made ice cream often. We had an old-fashioned ice cream freezer that had to be turned by hand. Mama made up the custard mix with our rich cream and fresh eggs. Often she added whipped cream, fresh berries, peaches, or other fruit, and sometimes she flavored it with maple and put in nuts. It was always wonderful. The custard and fruit mixture was put into the metal center container and the paddle slipped into it. The top of the paddle was square, and stuck out through the top of the canister. The turning mechanism was placed securely over the top of the square tip, and fit into grooves in the top edge of the outer wooden bucket. Next, layers of ice were alternated with rock salt all around the canister in the wooden bucket. When that was full, a gunnysack was folded in quarters and laid across the top. When I was little, I was elected to sit on top of that to weight it down; the men or boys took turns turning the handle until it would not turn any more. Then it was a rush to pull the canister out and take it into the house, where Mama cleaned the salt off the outside and pulled the paddle out. My favorite treat was to get to lick the paddle, but there was lots of competition."

CHAPTER 19

Bees

Nancy recalls: "Dad used to collect the honey from the beehives himself. He had a white coverall suit with long sleeves, and long heavy gloves, and a hooded head-covering with clear or screened hole so he could see. He used a metal pump can into which he put smoldering rags. He would pump the smoke into the hive to stun the bees, take off the top of the hive, and lift out the panels which were thick with dripping honeycomb. The combs were replaced with wax starter sheets, which had little six-sided dents to match the bees' construction, to encourage the bees to begin constructing new combs. The honey was delicious, and we served the honey combs right on the table." The bees had clover, fruit blossoms, all the flowers in the gardens and countryside, and I have never eaten such honey. When it was fresh from the hive, it was nectar. I could understand the Bible writings praising the "land of milk and honey."

Nancy learned all about this process by watching her daddy. "When a new queen would be born, a large swarm of bees would go with her in search of a new home. Where she landed, the rest of the bees would cluster all over and around her. There were always thousands of them. It was a real trick to capture the whole swarm and put it into a fresh new hive. The queen had to be captured or it wouldn't work.

"During the War, many things were rationed, especially those things which were either imported, or were needed to fuel or feed the war effort, like coffee, sugar, meat, tires, gasoline. Mama made much use of the honey our bees produced. She had a collection of sugar-free recipes. Substitute sweeteners were not nearly so available as they are these days.

"Kent and I used to kneel side by side on our knees on chairs at the big pull-out breadboard at the hutch. Mama would mix up an ample batch of ginger cookie dough, made with honey instead of sugar, and we would spend hours rolling out the dough and cutting cookies for her to bake. It was great fun. The last ones were pretty hard and dry, by the time they had been re-floured and re-rolled several times, but they were all eaten just the same. It kept us busy and entertained for a very long time, and provided snacks and dessert for everyone.

"Grampa Walker made games for us to play. We had a beanbag toss, and a croquignole board. I have the board. *(I*

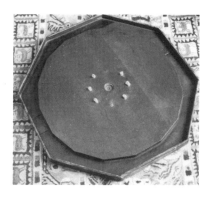

wish I did, says Jodie.) We played lots of games: children's card games, Chinese checkers, rummy. Dad and Norman and Edward and Grampa and Grandad used to play cribbage, and Dad always beat me. I won from Mama most of the time, but I suspect she either didn't really have her mind on it, or she let me win. She always smiled about it.

"Mama taught me to use the sewing machine when I was eleven, and she showed me how to read patterns. After that, I made most of my own clothes, using some new fabrics, and some of those pretty printed feed sacks. I learned to be proficient at mending, too, and could hand sew perfect buttonholes. When I got to college, I made my own formals for the dances.

"One of my very young memories is going with Dad to deliver the milk down on First Street, when it was just mud or dirt. After the delivery, we would pick up a huge block of ice to go into our icebox. I was impressed with the large tongs that were used. I don't remember when we switched to a refrigerator, but I remember a green one with side-by-side refrigerator and freezer doors. Mama always insisted that all the things to be put in be collected beside the refrigerator on the round kitchen table, so one could open the door once, quickly put everything in, and close it. That way the least amount of cool air would be lost—holdover from the icebox, maybe. One time, I had my hands full, and needed to open the door, so I took it with my teeth. The door handle snapped and broke a chip out of one of my front teeth. Mama was <u>very</u> upset!

"We had a cooler that was a tall narrow cupboard between the refrigerator and the outside wall. The outside of the cooler was screened, so the outdoor air could keep things cool. One year, when Jodie was in high school, and Archie Carlon was living above the laundry, we had a recipe for home-made root beer. We used the cooler for storing the bottled root beer. When it was ready, we tested it and thought it very tasty, with a much better flavor than the commercial drink. But then some of the bottles began to explode, which was pretty exciting while it lasted. We decided we'd better dump out the rest."

CHAPTER 20

Work Horses

There are adventures and exciting moments on a farm. We may think of it as a haven, and perhaps it ordinarily is, but there are some dangerous moments, too. Jodie was pretty much always around the barn and horses, and she experienced such moment with a workhorse: "Once Old Nell, the big mean workmare, attacked me — I have no idea why — when I was standing in the barn yard. She reared to full height and was coming down heavily, a frightening sight! I hurriedly stepped back, falling over the tongue of the big wooden roller. She came down and smashed the tongue with her front feet! That was too close! Mr. Dengue chased her off with rocks!

"So I wasn't too awfully upset when she got tetanus from poking herself on barbed wire while reaching over a fence to steal some forbidden bits on the other side. She died, of course, and no one else was happy because that was a blow to our Farm economy — we no longer had a team.

"Some men dug a huge hole down at the foot of the lane to bury her — she was <u>big</u>. Dad didn't like it that I went down to watch. He was frustrated and concerned at the loss. After that we had to hire Roy Kropft and his team of great dappled Percherons, Kit and Doll. I sometimes got to ride them when they worked — plowing, or hauling in the loaded hay wagons, and when Doll pulled the hay up into the loft with the big hay fork to empty the wagons.

"The barn had work horse stalls, cow stanchions, a grain room, and a huge loft (I fell out of the loft once onto a cow manger. All of us played in that loft.) The hay was loose in those very early days, not made into bales, and all was worked by hand with pitchforks. The drovers backed the teams into the opening with the big loads of hay, and unloaded what they could with pitchforks. Then one of the horses would be hooked by her harness onto a long rope hanging from a pulley at the top peak of the barn where there was a big opening. A large hayfork would be pulled down and clamped into the load of hay, barbs going down in like fishhooks. Then the horse was called to 'gee up' and pull across the yard. The fork would lift a shock of hay to the opening, where it hit a metal track and went sailing to the place they wanted it, and they would yell, 'Whoa!' and jerk a trip rope, releasing the fork barbs and dumping the hay into the mow. The horse worked this on command!" By the summer's end, the lofts were full, and the cows and horses were assured of winter food.

Nancy recalls with pleasure the haying: "I remember sometimes sitting atop Doll, the black draft mare who pulled the hay fork. Either Jodie or I would often ride her while she worked. My legs stretched horizontally across her broad back. Haying was a family affair, once the hay was cut, rowed, and dry, in the field. Our little cockers, Gretel, Honey, and Cherry, loved the haying, and so did the cats. They followed the wagons and waited eagerly, watching alertly—ears twitching—the layers of fresh-smelling oat and vetch hay being forked from the stacks, until the ground was bare and the mice who had taken up residence while the hay dried would scamper hither and thither looking for new hiding places. Haying season resulted in fat cats and panting dogs. The cockers would return to the yard when their job was done, stretch flat on their stomachs, back legs stretched out behind on the cement walk, and pant, smiling happily over the day's activity.

The fields were golden yellow and crisp after the hay was cut, crunching under foot and radiating reflected light and warmth. After haying was finished, the cows and horses were turned out to graze the stubble."

The cats were not pets, as they lived in the barn and were seldom around the house. But George, black and white and charismatic, became one of the children's favorite kittens. It came as a complete surprise to everyone when George later on presented us with kittens! She had more than one family, and somewhere down the line, Lauri and I came home with one of her descendants, a sleek panther-black female we named Twink, who also begat Junior, Lauri's all-time favorite. Junior was anything but beautiful, but she dearly loved him. Unfortunately, Junior looked like his father, who was the homeliest cat in the neighborhood, remarkably resembling Groucho Marx. Twink was beautiful, but had no taste and no morals, and eventually I gave her to a farmer who needed another barn cat, because she was a smart and excellent mouser.

Everyone on the Farm really worked, and Jodie described some of what had to be done. "I still got corralled into washing or drying dishes, setting tables, oiling and polishing furniture on Saturday, trimming off dead blossoms from flowers in the yard, raking leaves, even carrying wood — what a heavy job that was! We burned lots of wood in that big old house. We split and carried wood every day. Big truckloads of fir blocks would be hauled in from the mill and dumped in the play yard to season. Then it was split and stacked in the woodshed on the front of the garage or in small neat piles elsewhere. Small wood and building scraps were used in the garbage burner in the kitchen. After the fireplace was added to the kitchen, it was so cozy in there that the big living room wasn't used so

much, especially after we children were grown up and gone.

"After the big barn was moved, we stacked the firewood there next to it under the overhang of the roof, across from where Dad had the bird pens built. Edward had a big pigeon pen, with a little house and loft. I remember the mamas feeding the babies and how ugly I thought the featherless squabs were. We also had some chickens and beautiful golden pheasants.

"In those earliest days Mama did lots of washing by hand, and with the scrub board. We went through a series of washers, noisy wringers, and even a primitive spin dry. Our household enlarged when Grandmother Allworth became too ill to look after her home any longer and she and Grandad came and lived with us. Mama had three washtubs of water — one for clear rinsing — they were always full of bedsheets from Grandmother's bed, and there were always sheets drying on the line. Grampa made a great folding rack to hang clothes on in the house in the wintertime. I helped with the washing a lot, and hanging the clothes out. I still dry my clothes this way, and I also have Mama's clothes rack and one of her laundry baskets."

Grandad wore long underwear in the winter, the one-piece style. He was a big man, so when Ethel hung the clothes out to dry, it hung almost to the ground. In the winter, when she sometimes took advantage of a sunny day and hung the clothes out, they would usually freeze, and she just put that long stiff underwear across a shoulder and carried it in like a soldier would a gun.

"I do remember when Dad bought Mama her new electric refrigerator," Jodie continues. "He had it delivered while she was out for the afternoon. It had a great big red bow on it like in the magazine ads — big, white gleaming

fridge! When Mama came home that afternoon, we had to make up something to get her to come over that way—I thought she was going to faint when she saw it." We had come a long way from the little brown icebox. It was always Ed who instigated the improvements. Ethel seemed to cling to the old ways—it seemed to be a part of her psyche.

Among Jodie's early memories there were some favorite scenes, usually outdoors or around the barn. "When Dad and Grandad were milking the cows in the old barn, I would see the cats lined up to catch the milk that they would squirt their way. The cats had milk all over their faces and whiskers. We never bought cat food in those days! There were always plenty of <u>mice</u>. I caught a mouse by the tail one day and it *climbed up itself* and bit me between my thumb and forefinger. I let it go, fast!

"Early in the history of the Farm, we fed the harvesters, mostly the neighbor men who were driving their teams and running the big threshing machine. The women, under Mama and Aunt Edith's supervision, served the men on long plank tables over sawhorses that went from the cookstove onto the porch. The men washed their faces and hands from bowls of water that were filled and replenished from big pitchers. The old bell at the back of the house was used to call them in from the fields for dinner.

"I think there was only one threshing machine in the neighborhood and the neighbors took turns harvesting for each other. The threshing machine was stationary, and the horses pulled the mowers and rakes. The grain stood up in shocks to be picked up and taken to the machine. (Those old machines, the cultivators, plows, disks, seeders, manure spreaders, ended up in a pile over in the grove with the other discarded scrap metal, to be purchased by the dealers. They would be worth something now as antiques—people use them in their landscaping or in museums.)

"I remember Mama sitting in the play yard with piles of gunnysacks to mend, using the long, heavy, slightly curved needle. She cut some of the sacks that could not be repaired, and sewed them into small bags. At Christmas, she put unshelled nuts into them and decorated them for gifts. She also tried using the burlap as the base for her rugs in the beginning, but it was so harsh that it tore up her hands, so she switched to monkscloth. (She started with the huge monkscloth drapes taken down from the college's Memorial Union ballroom.) The most ragged gunnysacks were cut up to make pieces for mending the usable bags."

Jodie remembers with rueful amusement, "When I was quite small, there was a fish monger who drove a rattley little old pickup and sometimes came by the Farm. The back, or bed, was fixed as an open 'ice box.' There were all kinds of fish on ice, packed in neat groups and covered with newspapers and a cloth (those vehicles hardly went fast enough for things to blow out!). He had come over from the Coast with seafood galore. Mama would let me go out to the parking lot and watch while she made her selection, always alert for freshness and condition. It was exciting for me. One day there were fresh smelt and I saw one wiggle, and I said something like 'Ooooh, look at the little baby fish!' cooing over it, and the man gave it to me. I put it in my pocket and carried it around with me. A few days later everyone was looking around and sniffing and complaining of a strange odor. When they finally figured out I still had my 'pet fish' and spirited it away, I was crushed. I thought he was mine forever.

"Once when Delores and I were riding Dolly double, we rode over on the oak brushy Alnutt place across the road. We picked armloads of beautiful autumn leaves and took them home to our mothers (I was in about the sixth grade and Delores in the eighth). When we got back to the house everyone freaked out—it was all poison oak! We spent a week or so in the attic room recovering and being treated for a major case of poison oak."

Part III

LIFE ON THE FARM

CHAPTER 21

Bountiful Harvest

Jodie adds: "We began getting harvests from all of our hard work—fruit, vegetables, nuts, milk, butter, meat from the chickens and rabbits, eggs. I recall that we took food to some folks in town. The Starkers had a little two-acre nursery where the west end of Van Buren Avenue in Corvallis is now, and we took them food and traded for some shrubbery. They were also struggling at that time—no one could afford to buy ornamental shrubbery."

In the Fall, there were walnuts and filberts to harvest, and the whole family always worked on this, walking up and down the lane with baskets to fill. The little cocker dogs "helped," except they cracked and ate the nuts they picked up. The nuts were brought in and spread on large screen trays above the furnace to dry. When they were dry, everyone helped with the shelling. I remember that one year a thousand pounds went to Bursts' candy shop in town. Everyone in the family who didn't live at the Farm took home twenty pounds or so, and so did family friends. We also always shared in the pears, apples, grapes, peaches, and berries and flowers.

When the orchard trees matured and started producing, all of the family members had to learn how to pick and gently handle fruit, and Ed took boxes of beautiful apples, pears and peaches into town to sell. There was always plenty for friends, neighbors, and all the family. Two Hungarian ladies who had been refugees were invited every year to come and pick what they needed. They made Ethel a lovely stuffed wool comfort. Many years later, after the children were grown, when the harvest was at its height, little ads for U-pickers were run in the *Gazette Times*, and many people came out to get the fruit. One time a woman came with several children, who played happily on the swings and things in the play yard while she gathered fruit. Then she asked Ethel if she could just leave them there, since they were being so happy and good, while she went on about her errands!

Nancy remembers the berry patch. "It lay west of the big vegetable garden and in front of the row of poplar trees. There we planted a variety of bush and vine fruits. There were loganberries, two or three varieties of blackberries, red and black raspberries, currants, gooseberries, and two or three varieties of grapes. Mama used to pay me a penny for each pail of berries that I picked. The pail was the size of a Number 10 can (about half a gallon), with a bail for carrying. The cockers, Gretel and Honey, often went with me, and would strip off and noisily eat the berries on the lower vines. Many years later, our main source of berries was from the wild Himalaya and evergreen vines that grew around the Oregon countryside."

When Norman and I lived at Gilchrist, we came over for fruit and nuts, and many times brought our friends. We picked, and ate, and visited. And when we returned to the mountains, the trunk of the car would be filled with the riches of the valley—fruit, nuts, flowers, goodies. This was always such a joyous expedition. Lauri would play happily with her cousins, and Peggy and I would catch up on our family visiting.

CHAPTER 22

Cooking

Ethel made all of their butter while they had their dairy, and it was delicious and pretty, in little flower shaped pats. She made large bowls of creamy cottage cheese, mixed with whipped cream. (Connie Sample always claimed she gained five pounds every time she visited the Farm.) She made her own mayonnaise, so of course we all did, too, for many years, and the family was never quite weaned from that home-made quality salad dressing. She always made the maple syrup for waffles and pancakes, and she fried cornmeal mush in crisp cakes to be eaten with syrup, too. She canned many thousands of quarts of fruit, applesauce, green beans, tomato juice, grape juice, spicy garlic pickles, spiced crab apples, peaches, pears, prunes — all the largess of their garden and orchards. The little stone fruit house was filled every summer and fall.

In that kitchen there was historic cooking to match the *decor*. Many a huge turkey or extra large chicken pie, filled with lovely vegetables and big chunks of meat, and gravy, topped with golden brown biscuits; countless loaves of bread, all flavors, all sizes; pies, jelly rolls, cookies by the thousands, toasted cheese sandwiches, enormous juicy meat loaves that had much more than meat in them (Lauri insists she saw Auntie Ethel add some left-over fruit salad to the meat loaf she was making), potatoes *au gratin*, stuffed peppers, trays of toast (toaster was too slow), cinnamon rolls, baked apples, macaroni and cheese — all came out of that oven. Sometimes the biscuits were special, with a cube of sugar soaked in orange juice baked on top—lovely. Everybody in our family cooks just like that, except for the quantity. I make my toast in the oven, add extra things to my meat loaf, and do stuffed peppers the same way. I don't make my own mayonnaise any more, but Nancy and Jodie do. When I had a family, I made bread, too, and maybe I would now if I had anyone to eat it.

Farm Mayonnaise

All ingredients at room temperature. Beat one whole egg. Beating vigorously, add two cups of vegetable oil. Slowly add salt, to taste, one teaspoon sugar, a dash of mustard. Add one-fourth cup vinegar, slowly. SLOWLY is the key word.

I'm not sure that any of us would be able to write a recipe for most of that cooking, though! Once when Lauri called me to ask for the family recipe for macaroni and cheese, I had to make up a casserole of it to see just how I did it! We learned by watching and doing.

Jodie says, "Mama had <u>dinners</u>! I remember when we used the good china, we had to put a silver spoon in the cup before pouring the hot coffee into it, to 'take up the heat,' or the cup would 'pop' in half. We young ones learned how to 'pour'—fill cups and glasses, set the table, fill vegetable dishes, replenish butter, bread, jam, and jelly, whenever they got low. Oh, the coffee cake we used to have, on a weekend or holiday morning! It had lots of brown sugar topping. The recipe was in the little dark blue baking powder book Mama had of her mother's. I used it for years, and I used the popover and Sally Lunn and pound cake recipes in there, too."

In the keeping room the huge fireplace and mantel were surrounded with gleaming copper antiques—a warming pan, fire tongs, big tub for wood, a kettle filled with nuts and a nutcracker. On the walls were the wood racks of purtles, more hooked hangings, including the one with the Walker family crest and all the houses the family had lived in. (This irreplaceable hanging was totally destroyed in one of the floods later on at my house on Van Buren, a real treasure lost, made so meticulously by the only one who knew all those houses.) There would always be an exquisite seasonal arrangement—flowers in the Spring and summer, branches of tiny red crab apples in the Fall, holly or blue spruce in the winter months.

Another harvesting was the apple crop and the making of apple juice. Jodie describes it: "One year Mama pasteurized 60 gallons, corked the jugs and sealed them with wax. Dad invented a press using big blocks of firewood, a hydraulic jack, and squares of heavy gold-colored canvas. The apples were washed in one side of a double cement laundry sink, quartered to check for undesirable residents, then ground to a pulp in a commercial meat grinder. The pulp was then poured into the centers of the canvas squares, which were folded up, and four would be stacked between the big blocks of firewood, the jack would be screwed up, and out would come the juice down a spout and into a bucket. We all had turns at it and it went pretty fast. Ann, Delores, Celia, Lois and I, and probably whoever else was living there at the time, helped with the picking, bringing in, washing, and cutting, while Mama and Aunt Edith managed, pasteurized, and bottled the juice in the kitchen, and Dad, Edward, and the other men worked the press.

"Every morning like clock-work, Dad delivered the milk to the creamery downtown on First Street. The creamery belonged to Reimans, but it was a co-op. We hauled the milk in the back of the big old Packard, sometimes referred to as the Blunder Bus; in the 20s it was probably a luxury car! We had folding seats to put in the big space between the front and back seats for the family. I learned to drive in that old car, and on rare occasions, was allowed to haul my whole Camp Fire group in it when I was in high school." Someone told us once that <u>Hitler</u> had the identical model, and that it was sold for a prodigious amount of money after the war. Ed "sold" the old Packard, to someone who came out and took it for a test drive—and never came back.

CHAPTER 23

Horses

Jodie continues, "Edward and I started school in the Fall and rode to town with Dad every morning to Harding Elementary, because it was our school when we lived on Park Terrace. The second year, we transferred to Mt. Union Elementary in District 13 of Benton County. It cost extra tuition to go to town school from the Farm. We walked to school, of course, passing the Alnutt farm on the way. Mr. Alnutt was a ventriloquist, and delighted us by having the horse and trees talk to us as we walked by. Edward went to Junior High in town after one year at Union.

"I was sorry at first that we had to change, because when I went to town school, I was allowed to go to riding lessons afterward. But Dad bought me a thirty-year old white horse named Dolly. He traded a ton of grass hay to the riding academy for her. I loved her *with all my heart!* There was a photo of Dolly, when she was younger, on the wall of the riding academy office. Having my own horse surely took care of my out-of-joint nose when the two babies were born.

"There had been a black and white pony before that, named Peanut, but she was too much for me — stepped on my toes. Anyway, Dad sent her away and I remember crying as they were leading her down the lane. What a brat I was! Dolly was colicky one time and almost died. She was lying in the biggest front opening of the barn, and Mama spent hours holding her head in her lap and giving her encouragement, and she pulled through.

"Dad bought Edward a beautiful retired race horse named Slipalong. She was a golden chestnut, and when the sun shown on her it made rainbows like oil on water. I was supposed to stay away from her, but she would sidle up to the fence and I'd slip off the fence onto her sleek back. I could reach the back of her halter to turn her—we had fun when no one was around." That was not the only time Jodie rode without permission. When we still lived on Park Terrace, my sorority sisters told me that Jodie had found her way to the OAC Armory, and somehow had maneuvered the person in charge into letting her ride a big stallion—that was when the riding was taught there. If there were a horse around, Jodie would inevitably be on it!

"Dad's friend, E.B. Lemon, used to come out when I was little," Jodie told me. "He would bring his saddle and bridle to ride my horse. He had asked me if he could, and he insisted on paying me fifty cents an hour, even over my parents' protests. He rode really well in English style. His saddle was always polished and gleaming with the good care he gave it—he seemed to have great respect for it and he treated the horses that way—very quietly, I remember. He always was happy to ride and he brushed the horses, petted and thanked them.

"Through the years we had work horses, of course—Nellie was the biggest one, her sister Nell the sweet one, and dear old Molly, a bay with a white face, was blind. They weren't so large as the huge showy draft horses they breed now.

"For riding, we had Edward's Slipalong, my Dolly, QP—a bay mare who was half Hambltonian and half Arab and Welsh—we drove her to the buggy. A tall ex-jumper, Chief Joseph, the son of Man-o-War's brother, seventeen hands high, was bought for Dad, but Dad didn't ride him much because it wasn't easy with his stiff leg.

"Later we added Kent's Ivan, Nancy's Flora Campbell, and my beautiful Black Sadie. She was a thoroughbred who had been a polo pony until the war stopped all gathering. What a beauty Sadie was — swift as the wind, and all I could ever desire. What fun we had — and we never lost a race!"

"I almost killed my beautiful Sadie one time. I was riding over by Philomath and I saw a spiral of smoke going up into the sky. Instantly gripped in a cold fear for our home, I ran her out for at least four miles to get to a place on our road where I could see that the smoke was coming from a field. From my viewpoint it had looked like it was our house. I cried and became ill with relief. I walked Sadie until the lather on her was dry and she was breathing normally. What a great horse!"

When Jodie was 17, she was honored as princess at the Calapooya Roundup. She was also crowned queen at the first Corvallis Rodeo in 1947, sponsored by the local VFW.

"Dad loved horses," Nancy said, "and horses were my sister's first love. Mama also liked them, and had ridden when she was younger. Even during the last years she had horses, for Peggy and just for fun. She especially loved the tiny miniatures. We always had horses. The earliest one that figured in my own life was a white mare named Dolly. I was five years old when she jumped the border opposite the garage into the orchard and dumped me into the rosebush that grew there. I enjoyed the horses, but was not devoted. Jodie rode the countryside and made friends with everyone. Automobiles were yet young, and there were many folks who not only had used horses and buggies, but still had the buggies stored in their barns.

"Black Sadie, Jodie's beautiful thoroughbred mare, was her pride and joy. One day in the summer when I was walking in the lower fields, where the hay had been harvested, I headed down toward the woods near the river where I frequently went to gather wildflowers and watch the wildlife. Sadie was friendly, and I was unusually bold

that day, so I caught her and got on bareback—not sure why—maybe because I had never been allowed to. She was somewhat awesome; I must have been ten or eleven years old. She didn't seem to be upset, but she started to run, and we <u>flew</u> across that thirty-acre field to the woods at the other side. It was scary, but exhilarating, and when she stopped at the fence, I slid off. Having done it, I never felt the desire to ride her again, and I never told anyone about doing it until I lived in Texas, and Jodie and Evelyn came to visit. I told Jodie then, and she was amused!

"We still had QP. Her legs were a bit stiff, and her lower lip hung down, but her spirit was willing. We all rode her, and of course drove her, and had fun. The roads around the neighborhood were unpaved, so her feet and legs were fine.

"My own first real horse was a coal black mustang pony filly—refined and smart, who came to the college riding academy from the Indian reservation. She was three years old, and we named her *Flora Campbell*, after an English lady who befriended Edward in England during the War. Every day that first summer I would catch her, put on the bridle, and climb on. I had no saddle, but didn't really need one. Each day, she would buck me off, I would climb back on, and we would go for a ride with no further trouble. When after three months there had been no change in this routine, I wearied of landing on the ground, and we sold her.

"With Chief Joseph came an English saddle and a Western bridle. One time when I went for a ride on him, I picked up a canter, nice and easy, but the girth broke, and the saddle and I ended up in the dirt. I was still sitting on the saddle and Chief was cantering off down the orchard. I didn't become involved with horses again until my son Mark was eleven years old and decided he wanted to ride.

"I remember going with my parents to the Grange for meetings, food, and dancing, and Dad always waltzed with me. *(Ed was a good dancer, even with his stiff leg, and I also danced with him a number of times, feeling very proud.)* It was near the end for the granges, and there are not many left."

> *The Patrons of Husbandry, as the Grange was known, was an association of farmers, organized in the United States in 1867 by Oliver H. Kelley and six other men. In 1912 it became involved in cooperative marketing, and had a half million members in a political and economic program. Locally, Granges became a social as well as business center of farming communities.*
>
> — Quoted in part from
> *Ten Thousand Goodbyes*
> by Robert M. Morgan

"Kent and I walked to school when we attended Mt. Union Elementary. It was about a mile from the Farm. During the rainy weather we wore knee-high rubber mud boots, and it was fun to slosh along in the ditches beside the road. We had memorized where the places were that were too deep for the boots. When we all arrived at school, everyone's boots were lined up in the coatroom, and we wore the shoes we had carried to school. Wearing just socks was not good because the floors were heavily oiled and black, and it would have ruined our socks.

"One time Mr. Alnutt, who really liked Kent, gave him the biggest apple we had ever seen. It was a Greening. I asked for bites, but Kent said he was going to eat it all himself. Two days later he was still eating on it before he finally gave up.

"The farmhouse was the only home I knew until I was married—twenty-three years. How I loved the Farm. I wanted that time to never end."

Jodie shares that nostalgia: "It is late November 1998 as I write this. If I were back in time and home at the Farm right now, I'd be walking along, kicking the deep oak leaves out in the grove, stomping on the oak galls to hear them snap, collecting acorns and watching out for the best mistletoe for Edward to shoot down for Christmas with his 22. The outside faucets would be wrapped and tied with old burlap sacks to keep them from freezing, and we'd be gathering the last of the filberts off the ground."

Thanksgiving was celebrated in our family with deep and sincere feeling. Ed sat at the head of the long table and offered thanks. We had <u>so much</u> to be grateful for. After Dot and Otto were married, the family went there for Thanksgivings, and had Christmas at the Farm. Dot's Thanksgivings were splendid. Jodie says it was <u>really</u> Thanksgiving when Edward and Norman and I came home from the war. It wasn't too many years later when Lauri came to join us and melded in with her Linden, Lea, Gay, Ralph and Peg, Edward's Clark and Nancy's Mark, Katherine, Karen and Kent.

But the first Thanksgiving for Norman and me at home after the Philippines was at the Farm. It was so beautiful, so bounteous, and Ed's grace was so touchingly filled with gratitude that Norman broke and left the table in tears, overwhelmed with what we now had and what was behind us. He never quite relinquished the pain of losing the friends who did <u>not</u> make it home.

One other note of importance about that otherwise festive occasion: we discovered the huge tray of stuffed celery that I had prepared so carefully—in the refrigerator, <u>after</u> the dinner was over.

"Ed and I," Ethel's journal notes, "had a nice social life with all of the Memorial Union events. He also belonged to Rotary, worked for the Republican Central Committee and the Red Cross. I was an active member of the neighborhood "Sunshine Club" and Tuesday Bridge Club. Ed was always a superior citizen—in fact, a superior man in every way— son, son-in-law, father, brother, friend, and husband. One time Bob Ingalls, editor of the *Gazette Times*, told me that the local Republicans wanted Ed to run for governor of Oregon. I had to tell him that Ed's health was not equal to the many problems and burdens of government and politics.

"Every morning Ed, Edward, and whoever was helping at that time, were in the milking barn by 4:30 or 5, milking and doing the chores. Soon after that I, and my helper, if I had one, would be tearing around the kitchen concocting a breakfast of cereal, hot biscuits, eggs, bacon, or whatever, and filling at least a half dozen lunch sacks, each labeled because of different amounts — one sandwich, three sandwiches, always carrots, and apples for dessert and for  cleaning teeth. Everyone would come in from chores, clean up and have breakfast around the big dining table, with a fire in the fireplace if it was chilly, then off to school and work. I then began my day — washing, ironing, cleaning, mending, sewing, canning, painting, rugging, taking care of my babies, gardening, writing letters, visiting with friends who came or called, and finally wondering where the day had gone!"

CHAPTER 24

Help

Ethel usually had household help, sometimes family, sometimes the wives of the college students who lived and helped with the Farm work. Evlyn Frakes remembers, "In the Fall of 1933 I was living in a dormitory on the OSC

campus during Freshman Week. One of my roommates was Lois Metcalf, and we became good friends. Lois introduced me to Mr. Allworth, her uncle, who was Manager of the Memorial Union Building, where my boy friend, Maurice, and I spent a lot of time between classes. Maurice and I were married in November of 1934. Shortly after that Maurice told me that Mr. Allworth had asked him if I would be interested in working at The Farm, helping Mrs. Allworth. If that worked out, Maurice would work there also. I started immediately. We had the room over the laundry room.

"Ethel and I got along wonderfully. Maurice and I had never known people like the Allworths. They were always helping young people and making it possible for them to realize their dreams. It was truly a great learning experience for both of us. All the young people who worked there were treated like family. Maurice was given tuition and book money in addition to room and board. I was given a weekly salary for things we needed personally and entertainment, and room and board. We were there two and a half years. These were two of the finest people we have ever known.

"There were so many things I learned from her, and I was, and am, most appreciative. An impression not to be forgotten was that we never were to pour the juices from the cooked vegetables down the drain—she said there were many vitamins and nutrients in that juice, and it would be a shame to waste them. She didn't buy prepared baby food either. She fixed veggies and mashed them for the babies. She showed me how to make salad dressing—the family ate it on <u>many</u> things other than salad. I learned to make a special cake with applesauce, chocolate, and raisins, and I still have that recipe in my file.

"There was always washing and ironing to do. In those days we used cloth diapers. All the men wore white <u>starched</u> shirts. She showed me the best and easiest way to iron a shirt and I got so I could do one in eight minutes! There were no 'wash and wear' clothes, so everything needed to be ironed. Anytime I ran out of something to do, I could always iron.

"She spent hours hooking and braiding rugs, and she was an artist in her work, very talented. She also loved flowers and shrubs, and I can still see her out watering them by hand! We canned fruits and vegetables and made pickles, and loaded the fruit house shelves.

"Mr. Allworth's other job was dairy farming. All the fellows who worked there, plus Edward and Mr. Allworth, got up very early in the morning to do the chores. When the cows were in the stanchions and the bags washed, Maurice would come and call me to get up and get breakfast started. Ethel would come down in time to help with the preparation.

"I learned how to hook rugs and she taught me to knit— I've made many sweaters for family and friends. They had a Packard and an Oldsmobile when we were there, and when there was a good show in town Mr. Allworth would hand Maurice the keys to whichever car was available so we could go.

"I remember many times when the family all gathered in front of the fireplace in the middle of the living room. They'd talk and laugh and have so much fun. Some of the children would be sitting on the floor; sometimes Ethel would read aloud—there were shelves all around and behind the fireplace that were filled with books."

CHAPTER 25

Evelyn

I did not move to the Farm with the family. I was in college, and thought that to live five miles out of town, on a farm — of course, without transportation — would be the end of everything. So I moved into the Gamma Phi Beta sorority house, where I was a member, and there I lived for the rest of my school life.

Norman Whitfield and I became engaged, and in 1934, Norman and I both ran out of money altogether. There were few jobs available, and the future looked a little bleak for Norman. He was able to get a job on a President liner to the Philippines, where his father and stepmother, Ray and Polly Whitfield, lived. So Norman went to work out there in the lumber business with his father.

I went to live in Portland with my sister Dot, and found a secretarial working in an office. We had a tiny apartment, pooled our money, and had a good time. She sewed for me, so that I had a sweet if modest trousseau, and in May, 1935, I sailed out to marry Norman in the Philippines — but that's another story.

CHAPTER 26

Dot's Wedding

Dot married Otto in 1938, and they had a darling wedding at the Farm. She was so pretty in her soft pink dress and shoes to match. Our Dad said, "I never thought I'd have a bald-headed son-in-law," but bald or not (and indeed he was), the family took Otto into their hearts that July day. He was dear to us all, and so much a part of the family. He and Lauri were good buddies—he thought she was wonderful. He tamed his big voice for my quiet child, and she once said to me, "Mom, I couldn't do anything bad! I'd have to face Uncle Otto and Uncle Ed!" We were all important to each other.

In late summer of that year, weeks after Dot's wedding, Ethel says, "One day while I was busy cleaning in the living room, my 91-year-old Dad came in on the way to go down the lane for the mail, as usual. But he sat down in his big rocker and said, "Daughter, I don't believe I can make it." I looked at him, saw how white he was, helped him to his bed, and he died in my arms. I sent one of the children to call the doctor, who came immediately, but he was gone." Our Dad is buried at Crystal Lake Cemetery beside our mother— together as always—and his mother, Sarah. There are twelve headstones out there now in the two family plots.

CHAPTER 27

Grandad

Grandad Allworth continued to live at the Farm for years. He also loved working in the garden. One day a friend was visiting with Ed and remarked that was awfully hard work for such an elderly man. Ed said, "I'd rather have my Dad die working in the garden than lying in bed." When Grampa Walker was still living, the two grandfathers had many cribbage games, and very interesting conversations. Each of them would stand back to allow the other to go through the door first. Our Dad referred to Grandad as the "old gentleman." (They were both in their nineties.) My Dad was a staunch Republican, and Grandad was a Democrat!

Grandad Allworth was something of a scamp, deliberately tossing a burning brand into casual conversations sometimes just for fun. He was a large man, distinguished looking, with a stunning halo of snow-white hair. Born in Ontario, Canada, he had become a citizen of the United States, and had at one time been the editor of a newspaper in Jacksonville, Oregon. He had not been a gentle father or husband, but he was a keenly intelligent and interesting person. The children were fascinated by his habit of taking part of his teeth out, placing them in his pocket, before a meal. He never used sugar in his tea until there was rationing, then he suddenly began using two teaspoonfuls in every cup.

Ethel wrote, "Grandmother Allworth lived with us for awhile, but became so frail that she needed more care than I could give her. They took her home to Battle Ground where

she soon passed away. I loved her—one of the best friends
I ever had—a dear, very educated lady. One day when I was
bathing her little misshapen feet she explained to me why
they were that way: 'Papa drove the horses to Portland,
about 30 miles, to do the shopping. He bought shoes for the
whole family. We had to wear them whether they fit or not,
and they usually didn't.'"

VICE

Vice is of such hideous mien,
That to be recognized needs
but to be seen.
But too oft familiar with its face,
We first abhor, then endure,
then embrace.

CHAPTER **28**

Sayings

Nancy treasures the time when she and Kent were alone at home with their mother. "Mama always read to Kent and me. Sometimes, she would read to us at nap time, with one lying on either side of her. She usually went to sleep, and we would have to waken her to finish the story. She taught Kent and me to play the piano (and through the years to come, countless other children and grandchildren). She wrote out simple versions of her favorite songs and hymns and taught us to read the notes and chords and to play and sing them. Kent really didn't like it too much, but we sat on the bench, one on each side of her, and we all sang from the old books.

"Mama loved poetry and could recite all or part of many classics from memory (Grampa did this, too).

"She collected sayings, Bible verses, and famous quotes, and had a very effective way of passing on good and appropriate thoughts to us! She typed or wrote out the verses she wanted us to learn. The Lord's Prayer was at the left of the downstairs toilet, just above the paper roll. The 23rd Psalm graced the wall above the toilet paper roll at the right of the upstairs toilet. At the right side of the downstairs washbasin was posted the 'vice' poem, which I carry in my head still.

CHAPTER 29

The Fire

The old farms always had fires. The Farm lost its great old barn to fire, and had at least one small but potentially dangerous one in the house.

On Nancy's seventh birthday, as the family was all in the kitchen watching her open presents, and having cake and ice cream, the telephone rang. I'll let Ethel and then Jodie tell it: "On September 16, 1941, a neighbor called to tell us that he could see flames back of our house. We scooted out and Ed called to me, 'It's us, Peg! Grab the babies and your mother's paintings and head out the lane!' Ed put Nancy and Kent into the 1938 green Buick and I drove it two-thirds of the way down the lane and parked it facing away from the house. It was our beautiful new milking barn! It burned, along with the granary, pump house, shop, and tack room. A squad of WWII soldiers stationed over on Baldy saw it and came over and carried every piece of our furniture from the house down into the orchard. I remember how queer our grandfather clock looked standing down among the trees. Corvallis had no rural fire protection then; the fire department came to the grange corner and no farther, and sat and watched. They said the chief was out of town, and that was as far as they could come without his authorization. But the Philomath fire department came and finally the fire was out."

Jodie adds, "There was a calf pen with calves in it, and a storage shed for gas and oil for the cars and machinery, toward the back lane. The calves were destroyed when the gas tank exploded and the dairy barn caught and burned to its cement foundation. The Army squad, which was camped up in the woods, came *en masse* with vehicles and trucks. They rammed down the runway connecting the dairy barn to the big hay barn. They loaded up everything out of the house and drove it down the lane to safety. I kept water streaming on the garage a long time until the wiring to the pump house burned up and there was no more water. Terrible, frightening thing!

"The big barn, which was filled with 90 tons of fresh hay, did not burn, but there were cinders as big as a hand on top of the hay. When the fire was out, Bill Wolfe and I sat up the rest of the night to watch for any more outbreaks of flame. Neighbor Frank Watenpaugh stayed on the roof of the big barn all night, spreading wet sacks.

"The army boys returned <u>everything</u> back into the house as it was before, even to the change on Dad's dresser. Everything was perfect except one tiny finial was broken off the grandfather clock. They <u>apologized</u>! They had the piece. *We were so grateful to them.*

"The sadness was like a pall. The grain from the granary smoked and smoldered for weeks. I can smell it <u>now</u>, and it makes me sick. That was a terrible setback."

Nancy also remembers the fire: "I was so terrified I had terrible, vivid nightmares until I was in college and past. The smell of smoke still bothers me, and I was barely able to light the gas ovens when I took Home Economics in high school. I still choose to cook with electricity. The wonderful milking barn was destroyed. Dad had just had it completely fitted with new milking machines, and they were not yet insured. We had to keep someone guarding the sawdust pile east of the big barn for weeks, since it kept blazing up from sparks that smoldered."

So—no more milking machine. Ed had a big truck come to haul away all of the twisted metal scraps. Ethel remembers, "The driver saw our old ball and chain (Edward found in a vacant lot when he was a little boy) and asked if he might have it—I told him yes. After the fire we milked in the big barn, by hand. We had to milk the cows in shifts in the stable part of the big barn. It was very hard to keep clean, and lots less convenient. Ed could afford to rebuild only half of the milking barn, and it was a long time before we were able to have a milking machine again. The cement in the milking barn is pocked and chipped from the heat of the fire.

"I learned to milk — those <u>tails!</u> — I'll never forget them! We kept right on shipping our milk, Ed taking it to the Meadowland Creamery every morning on his way to work. I went on making cottage cheese and butter, which we often sold, too. We later made another change in our dairy operation, using artificial insemination for breeding instead of keeping a bull."

Jodie adds, "Many of the things in the shop that burned were mine. I lost my whole Camp Fire Torch Bearer art project, the beautiful old tooled sidesaddle Dad had bought me that had a seat made of rose-colored carpet — many many more things. But of course that was the least of the loss.

"During the War, I did lots of the milking. Kent and Nancy fed and cleaned up. Edward was called into the service as an officer, as he was in ROTC. Dad was pretty crippled up with arthritis in his old injuries. He had many wartime duties in the community also. But we delivered milk to town every morning because we had a contract with the Army.

"Finally, Mr. Kropft, who did our farming, bought a tractor, and the team was retired — Kit and Doll, dappled Belgian full sisters. Our own horses were long gone except QP and Dolly, the saddle horses. I drove the tractor some in the fields. Everyone was short-handed, with the boys all in the service.

"Dad at last gave up his fine dairy about 1948 when the powers that be said everyone had to have a $2000 stainless steel holding tank for the milk. We never had milked more than 28 cows at any period. Now we had only one milking machine, not enough income to warrant the big tanks, nor enough milk. I think it broke Dad's heart. One other thing — we children began going our separate ways, and there were no college boys to live upstairs in the garage apartment for their labor."

CHAPTER 30

Homecoming

The Farm had become a *mecca* for the townspeople, too. Mr. Hall's Junior High history classes were regular visitors because it was an historic site; garden enthusiasts came just to look and admire and learn, college groups, and friends from Corvallis and beyond, found their way to bask in the special hospitality of this place. The children were not the only ones blest.

Through all the years that Norman and I were away, so far away, we could rest our hearts and thoughts as we read the letters from home. Then when we returned from the war, and needed a healing time, where else would we go but to the Farm? There we picked fruit, gathered nuts, gardened; Norman worked on the fence and the little apartment above the garage, and I helped Ethel. I played the piano and sang for hours, learned to hook rugs, and brushed up on my cooking. After seven years of servants, and three

of the prison camp, this was a return to "normal" living.

Our homecoming in May of 1945 was a wonderful event. The war in the Pacific was not over, of course, so the wartime restrictions were still in effect. Gas rationing prevented any of the Oregon family from meeting us in San Francisco. My brother Kent and his wife Grace were there on the dock, and Otto's three sisters who lived in San Francisco, and my beloved Aunt Nellie, who was from nearby Alameda. After a week with Kent and Grace in Sacramento, we traveled north on a troop train with the GI's, wearing our army issue and little service badges, and being documented as "displaced personnel."

When we arrived in Albany, all the rest of the family was there—what a wonderful welcome! The old difficult years vanished and we were home and safe and there was so much love around that we were overwhelmed. We all rushed back to the Farm, and Ethel produced a memorable breakfast— memorable in more than one sense. During the last part of our imprisonment, when food rations were so minuscule, we almost never saw rice; our mainstay was cornmeal, very buggy. But one of Ethel's favorite and famous recipes was crispy fried cornmeal mush served with farm butter and maple syrup, and this she had chosen for our welcome-home breakfast! Norman and I were so filled with laughter at this un-welcome sight that we just couldn't contain ourselves, and my sweet sister blushed with chagrin. She was able to laugh with us later, fortunately. I still have no enthusiasm for corn meal anything.

Everyone we met through the months ahead would comment "Bet you're tired of rice, aren't you?" and we could only remember how we had wished for that nourishing food, which the Japanese had needed for their troops. We were grateful for anything to eat.

Nancy was a slim, braided and a somewhat shy, beautiful child, eleven years old—she had been in the baby buggy when I left home. Kent was tall, slim, handsome, charming and so excited at our arrival he could hardly hold still—he was almost thirteen. Jodie and Edward were no longer home. My father had passed away, and I missed him.

Grandad Allworth was there, and having a ball. One day he told some guests that a bunch of Filipinos had arrived and were staying at the Farm—meaning us. Another time he asked who Norman was, knowing perfectly well, of course, and then remarked to Norman's absolute delight that I must be a lot older than my husband! The five years' difference happened to work the other way, but Norman took full advantage, of course.

Grandad used to come in announcing that the play yard had a thousand cars in it—its capacity was four cars. But he moved one step too far when he told someone that our mother was the best Filipina who had come out of the Islands. Ethel's blue eyes had sparks in them that time, and she set him right very quickly—as I said before, he was a bit of a scamp.

Ethel wrote, "Polly Whitfield, Norman's stepmother, had been visiting her mother in San Francisco, and she took Evelyn back to the Islands, where they had a lovely wedding. Uncle Earle, Mama's brother, and Aunt Charlotte were living out there, and she prepared the wedding, and Uncle Earle gave Evelyn away; their three sons were the ushers. We were so sad we couldn't be with them, but so happy that Evelyn had family of her own there.

"They lived over there for seven years, then came Pearl Harbor and the Pacific part of WWII. They went through the tragedy of the war and were imprisoned by the Japanese for over three years. We didn't hear from them for so long—weren't even sure where they were—and when we finally did hear, we learned that they hadn't even been together. I'll never forget when we excitedly found Evelyn's first letter in the mailbox!

"Finally, the war was over and they were coming home—we met their train in Albany. There they were, Norman in a soldier's uniform and Evelyn in a WAC uniform with an 8-inch hem. So wonderful to have them home with us!"

When we finally felt strong and ready for the world once more, we moved away and once again, were gone for many years, but this time within visiting distance. Norman's first job was in Everett, Washington, where I found time to write my first book (*Three Year Picnic*), and was also able to fly down to the Farm for Jodie's wedding. When we lived in Central Oregon we not only came over often, but brought our new friends along, and they were welcomed forever into this always expanding family circle.

Leaving there was always a marvelous experience. The trunk of our car would be loaded with flowers, plants, soil; or apples, pears, prunes, grapes, berries, or nuts — whatever the family thought we could use or would like — *largesse!* The rear end of the car would be sometimes almost dangerously low! If we had not brought friends with us, there were always good things to take home to them. We would be warmed and filled and enriched from the Farm and the dear family there. No one ever left the Allworth Farm empty-handed.

Archie Carlon, who is now retired from the USNAF, and also retired from a business career in realty, found his experience as part of the Farm family "a chance to live." He was given a home, a small salary, and a family, during his high school years. He told me this had been a "great privilege." Ed found him at the Children's Farm Home, a facility for homeless children. He has been up twice from California to see me, and his memories of that time are warm and glowing. He also well remembers how hard everyone worked, and that he learned discipline from Ed.

One of the reasons they wanted to have a farm, Ethel said, was to be in a position to help college boys earn enough to stay in school, so there always seemed to be one or two living out there, and helping on the Farm, and Ed always needed that help. Quiet, capable Neil Hoffman worked and lived at the Farm while he was in college, and Lois was also living there at that time, helping Ethel and going to college. She and Neil fell in love, and had a pretty wedding in the backyard after they graduated. Lois was musically and artistically talented, and much admired and loved in the family. She has been my life-long friend.

She and Neil lived most of their married life in Eastern Oregon, where he served Oregon State University as County Agent. They have three daughters and a son. Neil fashioned marvelous coffee tables, bookends, and keepsake objects from thunder eggs, just for his own pleasure and to give to happy friends and family members. Lois makes fine pots and vases, and shares delicious dried fruits and nuts with family.

CHAPTER 31

Model A

Nancy says admiringly, "Sometime about junior high age I made the mistake of running when Dad intended to discipline me for something—probably being too slow to do something Mama had asked me to do. That was how I learned that he could run, really fast, even with his stiff leg!"

One of Nancy's fond recollections was of Edward's black Model A Ford that he had in college. She thought the car was "grand" and said that she and Kent begged to ride in the rumble seat, which was such fun!

She said she also especially loved Ethel's crazy quilt made from all shapes and sizes of velvet scraps, many of them out of our mother's clothes from a time when velvet was very fashionable. Ethel had painstakingly embroidered around the edges and sometimes in the center of each patch. Nancy liked to stroke the quilt because the velvet felt so soft and gentle, and she tried to memorize all the embroidery patterns Ethel had used.

She also thinks her father had been especially financially astute. "He was careful with everything, and we worked in many ways to keep costs down. All of the canning and preserving, keeping chickens and cows, and acquiring the skills that helped to make us quite self-sufficient, were a part of the economy of the Farm. Mama told me that Dad had refused to accept more than a very moderate salary for the job as Director of the Memorial Union. He said the job was not difficult. When he retired, the University had to advertise a salary of nearly four times what his had been.

"Each month, before he paid the bills, Dad bought a savings bond. He started with $25 bonds, and over the years, worked his way up to $100 bonds. With the investments and property he had acquired, Mama was amply supported for thirty years after he was gone, without worry for her financial security."

There was nothing penurious in this economy. Through the years, I thought Ed was the most generous man I had ever known. He helped countless college students, besides anyone and everyone in the family, graciously and without question. He took care of his family and ours, asking nothing in return. His wisdom in money management resulted from his education, his necessity, and it was based on the hard facts of the Depression era, when many people were in bread lines or on the street.

He approved of and assisted in Ethel's household economies. He told me that he never could have accomplished what he did without her help.

Nancy remembers that for some years, Ethel made her own soap. She had found a recipe, and collected drained off fat from those who didn't care to use it. She clarified it, and mixed in the lye, fragrance, and other ingredients, and left it to "set" in her enamel roasting pans. When it was firm, she cut it into big squares with a butcher knife. She used her soap to do the clothes washing and the dishes. During the war, this was a major saving.

She darned socks until the advent of nylon made it impossible. She seldom spent money during those years — but in later life, when she was alone, she supported and helped many of the young people in her family. I took care of her checkbook and bank account then, but she would never let me say "no" to anyone.

In the garage, Ethel had stored years of *National Geographic*, and *Life* magazines from the very first issue. When Norman and I came home from the war, we poured over those copies of *Life* to catch up on what had been happening in our country and the world while we were isolated in the Japanese prison camp.

CHAPTER **32**

Christmas

I am fairly certain that no other rite of the Christian world has been more minutely and variously described than the "family Christmas." From Dickens to Alcott, in poetry and song, in beautiful prose and common language, this is a beloved and poignant topic. Immortalized from *The Little Match Girl* to *It's a Wonderful Life*, with small drummer boys and Santa Claus all wrapped up together, and the Christ Child's aura surrounding all, Christmas is the most special family time of all. Lonely and alone people feel more alone than ever. Cynics believe it has been ruined by commercialism. Cries of outrage are heard when religious observance trespasses on "civil rights." Somehow, Christmas remains as dear and important as ever in the hearts of most of us, and we who have glorious memories of this beloved celebration are undisturbed by the detractors.

As you would expect, Christmas at the Farm was all it could ever be anywhere. The gala of it started long before the date arrived. Everyone made gifts, or shopped for gifts, and children with high hopes minded their manners. Food was prepared ahead, of course. Plans were joyously made, invitations sent, extra beds prepared. Jodie tells, "The whole family would go out in the old Packard to the hillsides to find a big-enough tree to fill the corner of the living room. I remember Dad's asking Mama to select the tree she wanted. Sometimes we'd get one so tall the top had to be trimmed, and we had ten-foot ceilings! As time went by the adventure fell to the younger members of the family. When it finally came down to Nancy and me, we really were picky, and trucked around in the snow behind Mary's Peak until we nearly froze, and it became a necessity to make a choice and get in out of the cold. We always had lots of boughs so Mama could make swags for the doorways, and gifts tied in bright ribbons with cones and berries, and to wind around the stairway railing. We had planted holly trees in the yard, so later on we had plenty of beautiful holly—also the birds seeded them from the trees over on the Alnutt place.

"Decorating the tree was a ceremony reserved for the eldest child, and I didn't get to help for the longest time. Edward did <u>such</u> a good job of it. But I could hardly wait. There were the old ornaments that came from time long past, looking very beautiful and Victorian and totally fragile—so many colors and types of them. There were colorful paper chains made at school, and popcorn strings, and other treasures. Over every branch separately were hung long shining strings of silver rain (then made from lead). Each year it was meticulously removed strand-by-strand and wrapped around cardboard holders so it wouldn't get tangled. It was the last thing on, and the first off, and lasted for all the years.

"I remember the loving Christmas care-boxes Mama packed for Edward when he was overseas, with tiny trees, holly, and cedar sprays among the gifts, along with nuts and cookies. They were sent to Evelyn and Norman in the Philippines, too, but none of them got delivered after the war started. I always knew that those boxes when opened up were wonderfully fragrant. Mama also fixed great boxes of candy and cookies to give to Dad's office staff at the Memorial Union, and to anyone who happened to be living in the basement there."

Once before the war, Ethel sent us by surface mail—no airmail then—a huge holly wreath. By the time it arrived a month later, it had lost its leaves! The pussy willows she sent fared better, and were a sweet reminder of Spring at home— lovely in my handsome brass Chinese tall vases on the mantel. A charming Japanese lady, wife of one of the carpenters at the mining camp, came to call on me, and was so admiring of the pussy willows, and with her limited English and my no-Japanese, I had quite a time explaining what they were. Ethel also sent us a wonderful big wheel of cheese, and that we could smell coming up the mountain trail to the house!

"Trays of candy were made," Jodie yearningly recalls, "fudge, divinity of all colors and flavors: white with nuts on top, pink with a maraschino cherry, green peppermint with chocolate dribbled over them. Oh, the aroma! Cookie sheets of candies cooling, and sheet cookies that you cut into squares after baking, with raisins and walnuts in them. Mama also made rocky road with nuts and marshmallow and melted chocolate spread onto a cookie sheet, and then cut into big squares. One year Uncle Lee Stidd brought a huge block of delicious dipping chocolate as a surprise, and that got to be a tradition. The block was about twelve by twenty inches, and two inches thick! We probably wouldn't have had rocky road otherwise. Our dear aunties and friends also brought fancy decorated cookies and gingerbread men. Mama loved ginger."

Ethel's divinity was unmatched, light, smooth, never grainy or crusty. Watching her make it was spell binding. There was just exactly the right moment for everything, knowing when the syrup was exactly ready, folding it into the egg white, which had been beaten to just the perfect stiffness, adding the flavoring and the coloring, at the optimum second spooning it out onto the buttered platter or cookie sheet. The coloring was especially suspenseful, as she added drop by drop the red (for a lovely soft pink), or the green (which must be pale, never garish). I have heard her gasp as she thought she had one too many drops! The result was exquisite. Then she would decorate the little mounds, and every batch seemed to be a masterpiece. I never saw her fail. And I never achieved that perfection, even though I use her recipe.

"Aunt Edith baked wonderful bread, and apple, pumpkin, and mincemeat pies. Before Aunt Edith came to live with us, Dad would stop at Gerdings' grocery store on the way home from work and buy big boxes of day old bread for about a penny a loaf. We used so much bread — for Welsh rarebit, melted cheese on toast, cinnamon toast, bread puddings, crumb-topped macaroni and cheese (ground up buttered dry toast makes delicious crumb toppings for all kinds of casseroles), a little in meatloaf to stretch the meat; sometimes for bean sandwiches to take to school. It took lots of bread for school lunches. We always worked hard and everything we had tasted so good!" says Jodie.

Lois said, "My daughter Lynne reminded me of the 'old toast.' She called it *Aunt Peggy toast.* Slices of bread were spread on large cookie sheets, then toasted in the oven and buttered. Leftovers were put in the hutch in the kitchen, where all the children could find it. 'Old toast' was never old, and everyone looked for it." It wasn't just the children. We all helped ourselves to that wonderful leftover buttered toast, with or without jam or peanut butter or honey! Toast was never made in the toaster — it was too slow, and the toast was not crisp enough.

A favorite part of our Christmas, to me, was the Christmas Eve party. Every year we invited friends, and anyone who didn't have a family or home, students, bachelors, older couples, to this wonderful occasion. Ethel would make huge baking pans of chicken or turkey pie, topped with biscuits. Sometimes some of the guests would bring cookies or candy. There was always hot home-made apple sauce, and apple juice or hot spiced cider or coffee to drink. It was just a visiting time, and very dear. Many of the guests would have had no other Yuletide celebration — many would have been alone.

After these guests had gone home, and the children and most of the rest of the family were in bed, Ethel and I would "do" the turkey. Modern dietitians would be horrified, but it was always perfect — we made the stuffing for the large turkey, filled it up, tied it together, and put it in the oven at about 200 degrees for the morrow! We had no idea this was not a good idea — the turkey was always delicious and tender, apparently harmless, as no one ever became ill. And that way, this big job was out of the way for Christmas morning, when we had breakfast and the tree to take care of.

My Dad was such a scholar, not pedantic, but filled with the love of old stories. Year after year at the Christmas tree, he told us the Christmas Carol story, so beautifully. The children felt a little impatient to get on with the presents, but we all sat quietly and appreciatively as he once again brought us a much-shortened version of that classic Christmas tale of *Tiny Tim*. At different times there would also be Grandad and Grandmother Allworth, Polly, Edna, Aunt Grace, Edith and her four girls. Archie joined the family while he and Edward were in high school. Bob Harvey was another addition for several years. Jodie found him living in his car, and told her Dad, who said immediately, "Well, bring him home." She did, and Bob spent years there. Long into the future, Bob never came to Corvallis that he didn't bring Ethel lovely roses.

Jodie recalls, "Christmas morning was unbearably exciting. Auntie Evelyn and Uncle Norman usually came down from the mountains a few days ahead. Our dear Auntie Dot and Uncle Otto and his daughter Shirley, and Uncle Windy and Auntie Mary, would arrive early Christmas morning, ruddy with cold, bells on — literally — laden with packages of gifts and more food — radiant smiles, laughter, hugs, hustle and bustle. The presents would go under the big tree, already stacked with them. The house was warm and beautiful and wonderfully festive in every nook and corner.

"Before we did the tree, we always had a great holiday breakfast, with hot biscuits and gravy, bacon (Uncle Windy brought delicious bacon every year, and Auntie Dot brought her delicious stollen, excellent plum pudding, hard sauce and glazed nuts), scrambled eggs, fruit, juice, coffee, milk, sometimes baked potatoes or hash browns, and Dad's prize recipe for cooked cereal, with real cream. He spent hours preparing that cereal, and whether you were a cereal eater or not, you did eat. It really was delicious, a mixture of Roman meal and other brown grains, dates, and brown sugar, cooked long and slowly in the top of the double boiler. We had such a good time eating and just being together that the little kids nearly perished at the delay of the presents!"

The tree took a long time. Each person opened and displayed each present, sharing pleasure and gratitude. There were always surprises, jokes, and touching moments. One year when we were living up at Gilchrist, I had made Raggedy Ann dolls for each of the small girls, and a Raggedy Andy for Ralph, and they were all sitting around under the tree. Another year each of the children received gay knit caps from their Auntie Dot. One year we all, without premeditation, gave each other really fancy embroidered fly swatters! I remember when I was still in college, and had few clothes, my gift was a smart suede jacket—I had never had such a luxurious piece of clothing before, and was quite overwhelmed. We never hurried—just savored the moment. Probably some of us instinctively knew how

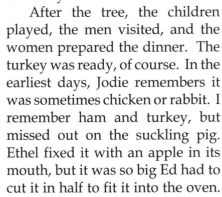

fleeting these moments are, and how they must be treasured.

After the tree, the children played, the men visited, and the women prepared the dinner. The turkey was ready, of course. In the earliest days, Jodie remembers it was sometimes chicken or rabbit. I remember ham and turkey, but missed out on the suckling pig. Ethel fixed it with an apple in its mouth, but it was so big Ed had to cut it in half to fit it into the oven.

When they served it, the split was all covered up with parsley and vegetables so it looked whole again. Jodie says "Yum! Later when I was older, Mama had me case the neighboring farmers for another one the right age and size, about twenty pounds dressed.

"Always there'd be cranberries in some form, ground raw with orange and apples and used as a relish; jellied, or sauced. There would be mashed potatoes, gravy, fruit salads, vegetables, yams or sweet potatoes. Sometimes Mama would have us cut little round balls of melons and fruits and serve them in a big crystal bowl of mixed juices, mostly orange juice. Dad always gave reverent thanks for our bounty."

Almost unbearably touching to me our first year home was learning that our Christmas packages had arrived in 1941 — I always mailed them very early, because transportation was by sea, and it took a long time for packages to reach the States. But the things we sent were put away when the war broke, because we wouldn't be there to share them — and in fact, by Christmas they had no idea where we were. It was so hard on the families at home! Ed showed me the finely monogrammed linen handkerchiefs I had sent, untouched and waiting!

The radio or phonograph would be on quietly in the background, playing lovely Christmas hymns and carols. But after Windy got there he would play on Mama's little black piano, and we had live music. We stood around the piano and belted out all of the songs we knew as long as he would play. We all loved the carols. Everyone in our family sang. Edward, Jodie, and Nancy have beautiful voices, and Ethel, Dot, and I always sang. The children grew up singing. Dad had a fine bass voice. Jodie reminisced, "I heard music from the time I was born. Edward had a band in high school, but even before that, he would play his guitar and sing in his room in the evening — the sweetest voice I thought I had ever heard. Like all the aunties and uncles and his mother before

him, he was in the operettas at high school.

"He played and practiced the saxophone and clarinet and led his band with a baton. When he was not at home I sometimes used to sneak into his room and

pretend I was leading the score of *Carman* with the baton—
we really had a workout!"

Ethel reminded me that Nancy had the lead in the college
presentation of *Oklahoma*, and it was lovely. She also soloed
for six years at the Christian Science Church when she was in
high school and college. I heard her fill the Coliseum with
her voice at graduation when she sang a solo there. She is
still singing, and it is still wonderful. There was so much
music in our family. We all played the piano, and Edward,
Nancy, Ethel, and Jodie played the guitar. Ethel told me that
Ed gave her guitar to her in 1930. He had given her one when
she was in college, and later she gave that to Lynne. Both
were Gibsons, and hand made. She played Hawaiian,
Spanish, folk, and classical, and loved to sing with it. Nancy
sometimes sang and accompanied herself at church. Ed
played an accordion, and had been an accomplished pianist.
Windy was a professional musician most of his working life.
We all loved hearing him play the piano, but I also remember
when he played trumpet and other brasses, and he began on
the drums! Jodie feels sad that she didn't do something her
daddy wanted her to do one time. He asked her to play and
sing for his Rotary Club, and she had such stage fright she
couldn't do it. But she sings for her church now, whenever
they ask her.

Nancy remembers: "During my five years of college, I
was privileged to sing in the concert choir and as a soloist
under the gifted hands of Robert Walls. In the summer of
1955, I auditioned for and won the part of Julie in a summer
stock production of Jerome Kern's *Showboat*. The performance
was at the Holiday Bowl, a large and deep excavation
located in what is now Lloyd Center in Portland. I lived
during that time in a boarding house in the city."

THE OREGONIAN SUNDAY, JULY 10, 1955

Starring in Kern Musical

Nancy Allsworth as Julie and Stanley Neuman as Steve, in the Holladay Bowl production of Jerome Kern's favorite musical, "Showboat," which begins its second week Tuesday at 8:30 p. m. C. Robert Zimmerman conducts the show.

A CORVALLIS GIRL, Miss Nancy Allworth stars in the current Holladay Bowl production of "Show Boat" being presented in Portland. Miss Allworth as "Julie" and Lenore Weller Leines as "Magnolia" are pictured above practicing one of the scenes for the popular musical.

Courtesy Corvallis Gazette-Times, 1955

CHAPTER **33**

Buggies

Another special memory Jodie has is of the time when she was about ten, and her daddy bought a horse buggy from Minerva Kiger Reynolds for $25. The Kigers were among the Benton County pioneer settlers. She says, "I had fun with that buggy for years. It has red wheels and hard rubber tires and a black body. My Camp Fire group would come out and we'd play cowboys and Indians. Someone would ride old Dolly, and some rode their bikes, and some rode with me in the buggy as I drove QP.

"Mickey Ball, my chum, and I used to drive way out in the country taking picnic lunches with us. Spring fever always brought us out, loving the beautiful countryside. QP was a small bay mare with back white socks and a bit of white between her soft velvety nostrils. Her black tail was slightly wavy. She always carried herself proudly. How she could trot!

"The second buggy was given to me by Mr. and Mrs. Black, of Philomath. It is a surrey with fringe on top! The third one Mickey and I found at the back of a farm place. It had 'trees' of wild roses growing all up through the spokes. We were told we could have it if we could get it out, which we did. It was black, and is what is called a *hack*. I still have it, and the surrey. The Kiger buggy is back with that family, on a ledge up in the seed company office, above the desk.

"One time I decided to hook up Black Sadie to a buggy. She was so quick, I thought we'd have a ball. I put the harness all on her, and she put up with that, so I thought, 'easy!' Of course the bridle has blinders on it—well, it was an old harness. I sneaked the buggy up and brought the shaves down and hooked them up. Just about then, Sadie moved her rear end over and felt the pressure on her side that she couldn't see. I never saw anything move so fast in my life! She shot away from there and the buggy never moved—every piece of harness that was hooked to it snapped. I didn't try that again. She was very good at what she did, anyway."

CHAPTER 34

Cockers

Raising cocker spaniels came naturally. Nancy says, "The dogs we grew up with were darling loving cocker spaniels. Ours were not the long curly-haired show type dogs that had to be clipped. They had shorter, almost straight hair, shorter but still curly ears, and the most wonderful dispositions. First there was Gretel, a beautiful, almost straight-haired, light red, love of a dog. She came to us a wiggly, rusty red sweet animal that spent some of the time then in the house. She thought she was a person. Her favorite place in cold wet weather was as close as she could get to the fireplace fire. I've seen her lying there, feet to the fire, <u>panting</u> from the heat and her wet feet steaming, but she wouldn't move. It was her spot.

"Gretel adored filberts, and when it was time to do the

nuts, Kent and I would sit on the floor with newspapers spread out not too close to the fireplace, and crack and shell the nuts. We had a small old piece of steel to crack them on with the hammer; then we would shell the nutmeats into a bowl or jar. We always had to put a newspaper under Gretel, because she so craved the nuts we were fixing that she drooled, and below her chin a small puddle developed as we worked. Every once in a while, one of us would feel sorry for her and give her a broken nut, and she would crunch it with relish. She stayed close to us as long as we were shelling nuts!

"When Kent and I went down into the orchard to pick up nuts to eat, we took Gretel with us. We gave her a nut, and she would take it in her back teeth and crack it, then drop it to select the nutmeat from the shells. As soon as she dropped it, we would snatch the nut and eat it. Now and then, though, we let her keep one. That way we didn't have to carry tools to crack the filberts, which have a very hard shell, and we let her have enough to keep her working at it.

"One memorable trip to the orchard," Nancy says, "Kent and I innocently chose to sit under a filbert tree that had a big nest of black hornets under it, which we never suspected. The hornets quickly became impatient with our being there, and came angrily zooming down on us. I had some stings, but they got inside of Kent's clothes, and he was badly stung. We were both in tough shape, so Doctor Tartar was called. We lay on the long brown sofa at the north side of the living room, Kent at one end and I at the other, with our feet together. Everyone was very serious.

"That hornet incident was not Kent's only brush with stingers. Mama said when he was quite small, he had wandered down to the bee hives, and climbed up to sit on one. When the bees began to sting, he kicked the hive with both heels, screaming and crying. Everyone was afraid to get near because the bees were so mad, but he did get rescued. He was taken to the hospital that time."

Gretel was the mother or grandmother of all the puppies that were sold from the Farm. Gretel never had time to realize she was a dog. The children dressed her up and took her for rides in the doll buggy, and she never batted an eye. Her puppies were in such great demand that there was always a long waiting list for them. Her puppies were charming, like Gretel—the wonderful disposition was almost always inherited.

Gretel finally had a helper, when her daughter, Cherry, also red, was kept and put to work. Jodie named her "Cherry Boots" for Edward's 'spit and polish' reddish paratrooper jump boots, and she was Jodie's dog. When she and Gretel had simultaneous litters, they sometimes swiped each other's babies while the mother took a break. They nested in the mangers in the barn where they were warm and safe. Honey was the other one, and she was Gretel's daughter, but almost blonde.

Nancy adds: "On one of my birthdays, my parents told me I could choose whatever I wanted from the litters of puppies. They were stunned when I chose a very light blonde cocker from a litter Celia and Arlyn had. We had been raising cockers to sell for years, but none truly blond, and Jennifer was. I thought she was so beautiful. She died at a ripe old age after Bob Ewalt and I were married and were living in Florida, and I cried and cried. (I was always so desperately homesick.)

"I remember a time in late summer at the Farm when Honey came to the door all caked with mud, and I hosed her off. She had been caught in a field fire when the Farmers were burning off the ryegrass stubble, and her hair was singed off. She went right back out and covered herself again with mud—I expect it felt good to her. Another time one of our dogs was shot, probably foraging too far onto a neighbor's property. She did recover."

Our "Gretel's Bamboo" was one of Gretel's puppies, and she lived as a precious part of our family for 17 years, Lauri's buddy, always sharing graham crackers; and Norman's fishing partner.

While Norman and I were recuperating at the Farm, he thought he'd do a little duck hunting, which was totally uncharacteristic of him—I had never seen him do any hunting of anything. He once told me that he would as soon point a gun at a child as at a deer. At any rate, he took the shotgun and Gretel, and went down to the river to look for ducks. When he quickly saw his opportunity, he shot one in the water, only to realize he had blasted a decoy. Gretel didn't go after it—she just turned around and went back to the house! Norman also came back, feeling a bit sheepish but most of all really so tickled at Gretel's disgust.

One day, when Gretel was pretty old, she came to the door to be let in. She did this once in awhile, would stretch out on the hearth rug in front of the keeping room fireplace, and just visit awhile. This time when she asked to be let out, it was her goodbye, for she was never seen again. Somehow this small angel of a dog knew, and took care of it herself. Several years later, Nancy found her under the laundry room. We did so love Gretel.

CHAPTER 35

The Little Rocking Horse

This is Jodie's story about the little rocking horse at the Farm: "This little animal lived at the Farm all the years. He is a 'hobby rocking horse.' Nearly every child in the family rode him—he has gone many a mile in the realm of 'let's pretend.' I was SURE that he was mine, but I have since learned that my brother Edward had ridden him first—then after me, my brother Kent, then sister Nancy! It didn't even stop there. Each one of my children is sure he is the owner, and probably Lauri and Clark and my sister's children.

This horse who has been painted many colors over time, had his first Christmas in 1916, under the tree for 'Eno.' He was bought new from the Corvallis Furniture Store by Eno's

father, Lee Stidd. When Eno outgrew him, Edward inherited the little horse, and he then spent most of his free time under our grape arbor.

Here in his 84th year (very old for a horse!) he waits to be painted again. He needs new eyes and mane and tail. The lovely brass stirrups are gone, also his ears, bridle and reins. The little saddle must also be replaced. He waits in the basement, and I WILL fix him."

CHAPTER 36

Hats

Nancy said, "Jodie and I were fascinated with Mama's hats and purses. She had two or three drawers full, and she enjoyed matching them with her different outfits. All of her clothes were feminine and dainty. Sometimes her activities reminded me of Victorian ladies. She had scrapbooks of funny cartoons, presidents, examples of pretty calligraphy, Native Americans, rug articles, garden ideas, sayings, design sketches—whatever seemed interesting to her, or of value for the future. There are also innumerable family scrapbooks she religiously kept.

"Mama loved pretty glassware, and had her collection spread throughout the house in the windows, where the colors sparkled in the sunlight or glowed softly. She liked baskets, too, and big ladles, and copper cauldrons which the family used as wood tubs by the fireplaces. There was a copper bed warmer Edward had sent home from Europe during WWII. Dad had a long handle turned for it. By the dining room fireplace hung a hand-made bellows with the Allworth coat of arms on it. Uncle Will had made it from alder harvested along the creek at Battle  Ground. Hand-painted metal trays lined the plate rail near the ceiling in the old part of the kitchen."

CHAPTER 37

Ted

Ted Hollingsworth, a buddy of Kent's, wrote about the little school he and our four children attended for a while—Mt. Union Elementary. "It had a steeple that once held a bell to be rung for classes to start. There was no electricity in the building, so the large glass windows provided the only light, and heat came from a huge stove that burned slab wood. An eighth grader was hired to come early and build the fire when it was cold. There were separate entrances for boys and girls! A playshed held the other classroom. Behind, in a grove of trees, were the two outhouses. The older girls helped the younger children. We thought it was fun to throw things at the outhouses when they were occupied!

"Water came from an old pump with a handle, supplied with a metal cup we drank from. We had desks with inkwells, and straight pens with which to write. We bounced each other off the 'teeter totters,' played softball, 'Annie-over-the-roof' (with the softball), and swung to death-defying heights on the long swings hung in the great oak trees.

"In my first year there, a large black car used to drive by our morning walk to the school, its driver slowing as he passed us on the gravel road. To a six-year-old the car seemed so <u>big</u>. The driver was Mr. Allworth, and the young boy and girl in the car were Kent and Nancy, on their way to Harding School in Corvallis. There were milk cans tied to the platform in the back of the car, from the Allworth dairy.

"At the start of school my second year, Kent and Nancy entered as new students, brought by their parents. They were acquainted with some of the kids, so were not complete strangers. Kent was a different kind of person than I had met before. He had an expressive face and laugh, and was fun to play with in games, real or make believe. Everyone liked him. There was an equality about our friendship in sharing, talking, games, mischief. I don't remember competing, just a mutual sharing and acknowledging each was good at some things and not at others. As all boys of that age during the war we drew endless pictures of airplanes on the chalkboard and paper. Kent was good at it. We read and shared lots of comic books—Kent had the most amazing array of them—and a collection of toys in his room. I don't remember Peggy ever having to settle a fight between us or send me home.

"I really liked the people at the Farm, and always hoped I wouldn't make a pest of myself. Kent and I belonged to Mrs. Lundee's Cub Scout Pack and earned our badges together. Mr. Lundee made us wooden models of guns in his shop and we spent a lot of time chasing and shooting at each other. Peggy took us on field trips—the one to Horner Museum was my first. My memories are ones of such pleasure: playing and learning together, being cooperative, respectful, friendly to each other.

"I was always aware that Kent was mindful of the chores he had to do. They had to be done without regard for whatever else he was doing or wanted to do. His father expected the work to be done, period. My father had chores for me but since we didn't live on a farm they were a different kind and amount. Kent had more to do than I did. Each of us had particular ones we disliked.

"We used to play in the orchard next to the driveway, and sometimes found ourselves at some point at the fence that kept Mr. Watenpaugh's turkeys penned in. We couldn't resist yelling at them or throwing something that would excite them into strutting and gobbling with fright, and we would laugh hilariously, of course, but always kept alert that no one was watching. We took walks into the eastern field and down to the river when the older Burright boys and others were duck hunting.

"The huge loft in the barn was a great place for Kent to practice his basketball. He did this with much purpose, and more skill that I had. But we took turns doing the shooting, running, dribbling, passing. He played basketball on the team at high school, and I thought it was from this concentration and practice, rather than natural ability. I felt it was something he really wanted to do well.

"The Farm had so many good places to play. On one side of the house there was a sand pile where we played war games with our toys. There were huge oak trees, places in the horse barn, lots of pasture and open area where we could shoot our 22s or BB guns. It had its own magic and romantic qualities about it. Many years later in Washington D.C., I saw a museum exhibit of the "Great Houses of Great Britain" and I was reminded of the Farm. Through my young boy eyes, it was beautiful, gracious, and comfortable. The kitchen seemed large to me, and quite different from the one at my house. Peggy would fix sandwiches for us.

"We kids liked Kent, and so did the adults. He liked everybody, and you knew it by his engaging smile, his expressive face and his charm. There was a sincerity and integrity about him. He accepted you for what you were. He liked to laugh and have a good time, but he had a very serious side.

"About 1943, Mt. Union School District consolidated with Corvallis, so those of us attending the school now rode the bus to Corvallis, and Kent and I went to Junior High. The large school made a difference. But my memories of this wonderful place and of my friendship with Kent and his family are always precious to me."

CHAPTER 38

Nancy

Nancy laughs when she tells about the slide. "When we were children, we had a slide at the Farm that had been given to Dad when it was taken down from the old high school, where it had been a fire escape. There were three 20-foot sections of U-shaped heavy galvanized metal, plus top and bottom pieces. Dad had a tower constructed above one of the chicken pens, with a vertical ladder which went up the side of the pen to a flat landing on top of the pen, turned left up a second ladder to the seat at the top of the slide. We used only two of the sections. There was much glee and fun sitting on pieces of cardboard when the slide was hot from the sun, or sitting on pieces of waxed paper to make the slide faster. The more times we went down, the slicker it became. When the going was good, you might shoot twelve or fifteen feet out into the field. It was a special thing for the time when kids came out to play. The chickens didn't enjoy it much.

"During the War, we children had little books that had pictures showing the shapes and ID markings for all of the American and enemy airplanes. We were to be familiar enough with them so that if we saw one that didn't belong here, we could recognize and report it. There had been some Japanese fighter planes spotted on the West Coast. Jodie was an airplane spotter.

"Behind the laundry room Mama had a short hedge of lavender bushes. She would harvest the lavender when it was in bud, and dry it. She sewed dainty small organza sacks, and filled them with the dried lavender stems and buds, then tied them closed with narrow satin ribbons. She slipped one or two into each clothing drawer, and sometimes gave them for gifts. The clothes smelled so lovely. I've tried unsuccessfully for several years to grow lavender, but I am determined, so I'll keep trying.

"I had many fields of interest very early, but my major love was wildlife, especially the flowers. I sought them out, brought bouquets of them to Mama, identified, took pictures and drew pictures of them, and dug them to plant in the "forest." The forest was much too dark and dry for them, of course. I spent many quiet hours walking through the woods and fields on our farm and in the neighborhood.

"There are pictures of me at this age in the scrapbook with straight loose hair. But in grade school I was always in French braids. Mama would braid my hair so tightly that it pulled my eyes back like Asian eyes! Usually the 'do' would last for two days. I wore a ribbon tied around the rubber band that held each braid, and had lots of beautiful different ribbons. Mama fixed my hair this way until I was in the 6th grade, and then I was allowed to wear it down—so grown up. One time one of the boys in my class pulled my braids down so hard that my head was almost on his desk. I turned around and hit him hard, just as the teacher-principal came in the door. It didn't take her long, however, to figure out exactly what had happened.

"When I was twelve, Professor Bill Kirkham, a friend of my family, opened an ice-skating rink in Corvallis. I had a new pair of skates, and went skating whenever I could. I loved it, and wished I could do it more. (When it got cold enough to freeze—which wasn't very often—the standing water across the road on the Alnutt place, I would walk over, put on my skates, and skate around the weeds and branches which held the ice up under my weight.) I still have the skates! The ice rink was not well patronized, and didn't stay open very long. Most folks didn't have much money to spend on recreation.

"In the oak yard by the new clotheslines, there was a high swing we called the 'big swing.' The swing wasn't so high off the ground, but it was fastened by great ropes to a very high branch. When you could get someone to push you, or you could pump hard enough, you almost felt you could fly out into the field! We never did get it up to horizontal, but we certainly tried.

"Kent and I played a lot in the hay loft. One time when some of the hay had been used up, we were playing hide and seek in the barn, and base was up in the loft. I was trying to hurry up one of the vertical ladders to get to base, and grabbed some hay with the rung. My hand slipped, and I fell onto an old wooden door which was lying on the ground below. My arm hurt, and I wanted to go into the house. Kent was mad at me, because he didn't want to quit playing, but I went anyway. Jodie was having a slumber party, so I just went in and lay down on the sofa. One of Jodie's friends saw me and asked Jodie what was wrong with me. Mama came, and took me to the doctor, who saw immediately that my arm was broken.

"When we were older, Kent and I played basketball up in the loft when it was empty. This must have been when we were in high school, because Kent was on the team, and he had me help him practice.

"The main chicken house had a side door, and there was a big fenced yard they could use in good weather. Dad sometimes got big boxes full of chicks from the Hansens, who had an internationally-known chicken business (White Leghorns). When the chicks were sorted for shipment, the roosters were either destroyed or given away. We had some hens, but the roosters were for eating.

"After the roosters were killed, they had to be scalded so the feathers would come off more easily, and I often helped pluck them. When I was older, I did all the plucking. Mama would cut and clean them to fix for dinner—we usually did three at a time—and that helped when meat was nearly impossible to get during the War.

"Every morning while the War was going on, Dad ran up the flag on the upstairs balcony, and took it down at night. Because he had fought in the first World War, it must have been very hard for him to have a son in the second one. The folks kept very close track of all the newscasts and newspapers. Edward was in such danger all the time when jumping (he was an officer in the paratroops). They were sick over the capture of the Philippines by the Japanese—Evelyn and Norman were in prison camps there. They longed for letters that never came; when one finally arrived after the war had been waging for more than two years, the censors had holes cut in it.

"We always had lots of candles around the house. Mama loved the brass candlesticks, and she collected them and candelabras. They also served to provide light when the electricity went out. The longest power outage I remember was two weeks. We also kept kerosene and oil lamps for emergencies, and flashlights. We could cook in our fireplaces and on the garbage burner when the electricity went out.

"Dad had a stand-up shower put into the downstairs bathroom so Grandad could shower. When he became so unsteady that he needed help, Dad would get into the shower with him to support him and be sure he got clean. It was quite an ordeal, as Grandad was pretty crotchety. The noise was terrific—two big men in a small shower stall with metal walls.

"Grandad was not always kind to Mama. He accused her of hiding his shoes so he couldn't take his walks. He regularly reported to Dad that 'Peg has stolen my socks again!' His walks were a problem. Once he encountered gypsies, and allowed the women to pet and stroke him, and he lost his wallet. Other times he walked too far and would be too tired to return, so he would sit down beside the road until someone came for him, or a neighbor recognized him and brought him home. A few times a stranger picked him up, and asked him where he wanted to go, and he would say that his son worked at the MU, and he was trying to get there. The kind stranger would take him up to the building—he actually did this a few times.

"When Grandad wanted to sit down, he would back up to his armchair, then allow himself to fall into it—he was heavy. One time when he had sat and dozed for a long time in a chair at Auntie Glad's, he got up to do something, and they found a mashed kitten in the chair. Apparently he never felt a thing!"

Nancy continues, "About the time I was in junior high, the folks developed a picnic area in the oak grove west of the garden space, beyond the Damson plum trees. A stile was built over the fence, and there was a big picnic table with benches attached, and a place to barbecue. It was never used as much as anticipated because by evening when we were ready to relax, and were home from work and school, the sea breeze made it cool and windy. The wind did keep the yellow jackets away, but still it was not very comfortable. There was also the problem of the Larsons' burning their turkey residue, which seemed to us most of the time, blowing our way!

CHAPTER **39**

Trees and Gardens

The largest trees on the Farm are the original white oaks. The grove on the west side and the huge oaks around the yard are grand. The largest one is in the 'oak yard' and there are two more at the east end of the play yard, and two more by the barns. Nancy says, " I used to collect the acorn caps and sometimes the acorns, because they fascinated me. Little crafty things could be made from the caps. During summer, we found yellowish speckled hollow puffballs on the back of some of the leaves. If you picked the leaf and put it on the ground and stomped on it, there was a loud pop. We had been told that the puffs were caused by insects, but we never found the bugs, and popping them was fun.

"At the south side of the property, between the oak grove and the barns, Dad planted Lombardy poplars. These trees have grown huge, and always brought a lump in my throat when I'd see them, after I'd been gone, because I knew then how close I was to being home. We used them to direct people to the Farm who didn't know how to get there, because you could see those tall trees touching the sky from over a mile away.

"Many of the trees that were planted around the Farmstead were flowering trees. There were ornamental cherries, crabapples, syringas, dogwoods, plums, hawthorns, golden chain, catalpas, magnolias, and tulip trees. Around all these trees were flowering shrubs as well: several kinds of spiraeas, lilacs, flowering quince, forsythia, flowering peach and almond, hydrangeas, bush peonies, lots of bush and climbing roses, beauty bushes, rhododendrons, azaleas, and laurels and privets. It was bee heaven!

"In contrast were the many evergreens: fir, cedar, pine, spruces, holly, and madrona. The English laurels grew as tall as trees, and had to be cut back to save them from breaking under heavy snow. There were both sequoias and big trees, the two kinds of redwoods. In the forest, all of which was planted as tiny seedlings, were different varieties of cedars and pines. We lost the lovely white pines, because we had currants planted in the berry patch, and they are the alternate host for a blister rust that attacks white pine. We didn't know.

"On the west side of the forest there are three Chinese chestnut trees. The nuts were inside of the prickliest hulls. I used to wear gloves to touch them. I tried very hard to think of something I could make from them, but I never came up with any ideas. We didn't use the nuts, either.

"Down each side of the lane we planted English walnut trees, and they formed a canopy across the lane. We gathered and sold the nuts, and used many of them.

"Near the property line at the foot of the forest was a clump of huge Balm of Gilead, or balsam, trees. The fragrance was so wonderful when the leaves were new that I used to go down there just to smell them. Mama said that Grampa had planted them. We also had some down at the river and along the drainage ditch.   "In the Fall, we were treated to the brilliant orange and reds of the scarlet and red oaks, the yellows of the sycamores and maples and the deep tones of the purple plums. We had mountain ash trees that bloomed near the picket fence, but the main show was in late summer, when they were covered with orange-red berries. When the berries were just right, in would come large flocks of cedar waxwings, and they stayed in or near the trees until all the berries were gone. They are such elegant birds!

"We had a Hyslop crabapple tree in the orchard. Mama made and canned yummy spiced apples from the fruit, to be eaten with ham. At the west end of the garden were the Damson plum trees.

"All along the west side of the lane from the shop and to the end of the front yard, Mama had more flowers and flowering shrubs. Here she had roses, daylilies, lilacs, flowering quince, spireae, forsythia, a large clump of nandina, hollyhocks, rabbit ears, saxifrage, iris, peonies. It wasn't always easy to pick up the walnuts while trying to avoid stepping on the flowers, and dodging the thorns of shrubs and roses.

"On the south side of the milking barn, after the fire and rebuilding, and between some of the tall poplar trees Dad had planted for a windbreak, were several artichokes. Often we forgot about them, and they got too ripe to eat, but when we did remember them we had them simmered and cooled, then dipped the leaves in home-made mayonnaise. When the plants bloomed, they looked like giant thistles, with beautiful purple blossoms, and sometimes Mama would cut them for her bouquets. The honeybees from the hives, and busy bumble bees, could always be found busily working them over.

"Probably Mama's favorite of all flowers was the violet. We had them in many different colors tucked into shady nooks around the yard. A huge bed of purple violets bloomed through the years under a great old cedar tree. Sometimes before the ones in the yard bloomed, Dad would bring Mama a little nosegay of purple violets surrounded with white lace, sometimes with tiny pink rosebuds in the middle, from the flower shop. He kept her supplied with cologne, perfume, and dusting powder called *April Violets* made by Yardley. This was her fragrance, and I never see or smell violets without thinking of her.

"Early in the Spring, I often went with Mama to Pilkingtons' nursery, east of town and near the river, where she would select English primroses and pretty pansies for her Springtime yard. Mrs. Pilkington and her daughter managed the nursery, nestled against the big leaf maples that hid the river. Some of the maple leaves were over a foot across, and we children sometimes used them for hats or play umbrellas on twigs. There were ferocious watch-geese which were not to be tampered with, and whom we treated with great respect. *(I was afraid of them – they were worse than dogs! Evelyn)* There was a slough that lay near the river that fascinated me, with many frogs, and small fish that would break the surface to catch bugs, and there were lots and lots of yellow dock lilies. Mama's favorite pansies were the blue ones with dark faces, while mine were the bright yellow ones with dark maroon faces.

"After WWII, when Camp Adair was closed and the area was quiet, Tom and Evelyn Wolfe took Mama and Dad and me out to the camp area to dig shrubs, plants, and trees. Tom, a retired colonel, had a pass. While Adair was active during the war, all the homes around it for some distance were taken over by the military and vacated, and the yards were sometimes filled with wonderful things that survived the years of abandonment. We found lilacs, viburnums, irises, lilies, spiraeas, peonies, laurels, junipers, roses, clematis, and brought them to our yards. We always seemed to be planting something, and we were aware that those plants would have been wasted.

"Mama had another large flower bed in back, much like an English garden. She cut many of her house bouquets

from this garden, and I remember clarkia, salpaglossis, snapdragons, cosmos, zinnias, marigolds, columbine, bachelor buttons, daisies, phlox, cleome, sweet williams, pinks, wall flowers, sweet alyssum, day lilies, peonies, coral bells, nasturtiums, violas, dusty miller, rabbit ears, anemones, lilies, saxifrage, delphiniums — all the beautiful summer annuals and perennials. In Spring there were daffodils, tulips, lilies of the valley, blue scillas, and grape hyacinths.

"For some years, Dad grew lovely gladiolus, which made gorgeous bouquets. After I had been to Hawaii between my junior and senior college years, I loved wearing the blossoms in my hair.

"Every Memorial Day, Mama prepared large bouquets of her beloved flowers to put on the graves in the family plot at Crystal Lake Cemetery. We would take lilacs, irises, peonies, and snowballs, and whatever other flowers would be in bloom at this time. The flowers were put into #10 cans or something as large, filled with water, and placed at each headstone. The little white marble headstones were scrubbed, and the weeds around the plot were pulled. Then as we crossed the bridge over the river on our way home, we would each drop a rose into the river for those lost at sea.

"The clematis came in many different colors—purple Jackmanii covering the little arched gate in the picket fence west of the sewing room, white ones with enormous blossoms elegant for bouquets, lavenders and pinks, and the fragrant, diminutive Montana climbing over the rock wall in the back patio outside the dining room windows. Of course I've always loved plants and flowers—they are so much a part of who I am.

"Mama grew lots of roses. For a time, her main rose bed was on the plot between the pump house-milk house-shop building and the milking barn, where the old granary had stood before the fire. The cement piers that had supported the granary were still there. She also had roses in the back yard along the house, including a big President Lincoln (so brilliantly red, so fragrant) given her by Mr. Hall after my brother Kent died in a car accident. Roland Hall was a middle school teacher who had been especially close to our family, and taught, at one time or another, most of us. He often, during many years, brought his entire history class out to see the Farm and hear the stories that Mama could tell.

"There were several bushes of old fashioned moss roses that interested me with their fuzzy frilly buds and sepals, and cabbage roses, rarely seen any more. My favorite of all was the Cecil Bruner climbing rose that covered the trellis on the south end of the gable, and the outside of the furnace room and sewing room. There was one climbing over the stone fruit house as well. The miniature pink roses looked to me exactly like the big tea roses, but tiny and adorable. I often wore two or three in my hair.

"Dad had a prize collection of lovely camellia bushes. Camellias do very well in the wet climate of Western Oregon, and Dad had gathered many varieties. During blooming season, the big radiant flowers were all over the house, and Mama would wear one on her suit or dress. Sometimes, when an especially lovely one fell to the ground after a heavy rain or strong breeze, she would float it in a flat bowl of water for a table display. Dad used to pick a favorite bloom and bring it to Jodie for her hair.

"Mama kept fresh flowers in the house all through the blooming season. She had a few varieties of winter bloomers, including Christmas Rose (Helleborus) that she used also. She would cut bouquets of English and American holly in the winter when the berries were bright red. In the Fall, she often had Dad or me or someone else tall enough cut small branches from the crabapple trees, before the little red apples fell, and she would trim off all of the leaves and make wonderful arrangements of nothing but branches of these clusters of tiny red apples.

"She used cedar branches that were covered with little bitty cones. Sometimes she used Fall leaves, and the leaves were beautiful but not very satisfactory because they didn't last very long .

"Another collection Dad had from which flowers were frequently cut for the house included many varieties and shades of lilacs. The fragrance of these was so wonderful, and the big bouquets were elegant and impressive. From snowy white through shades of pink, lavender, and blue, to the darkest violet and maroon, they were exquisite, and they were special to Dad. Some had heavy, double blossoms; some were old-fashioned and delicate.

"Eventually, Dad had a greenhouse built on the roof between two of the gables. The entry was from the upstairs hallway to the south, where there had been a window. We had a difficult problem with too much heat reflected from the two sides of the roof, and we had to try many ways to solve that. For a time I had it full of African violets, all types and colors. Later I made a good collection of orchids and tropicals, and some cacti. It was pretty special, even with its problems. We had a small electric space heater to keep the plants from freezing. <u>Someday I know I will have a greenhouse again!</u>

"The vegetable garden was grand. Grampa started it, of course, and it grew to rows of Kentucky Wonder pole beans, yellow crookneck squash, cantaloupe, acorn squash, huge Hubbard squash, carrots, beets, peas, corn, tomatoes, turnips, onions, dill, cucumbers, and other veggies. Mama canned over a thousand quarts of vegetables and fruits each year. I can't just remember where they were planted, maybe in the berry patch, but we had huge clumps of rhubarb. Kent and I loved to pull a stalk, break off the leaf, and chew the stalk—it was <u>so</u> sour. Mama made rhubarb sauce, like applesauce, and canned it. We used it for fruit; sometimes she made cobbler with it.

"The best apple sauce and apple pies were made from the Gravenstein apples. The yellow transparents were the earliest apples to ripen but were best eaten a tad green, since they tended to get soft and pithy as they ripen. We enjoyed applesauce made from them, especially because it was the first of the season.

"Many hours were spent snapping and pulling strings from the beans, peeling apples, pears, peaches; pitting plums, prunes, and cherries. The grapes were made into juice or jelly; berries were canned or made into jam; prunes were canned or dried. Dad hired the drying done by a commercial dryer, since we didn't have a dehydrator. It is nearly impossible to pit the sour pie cherries without missing at least one pit per quart jar, and it was a family funny that either a guest or Dad found the one pit in his piece of pie. We had gooseberries, because Dad loved gooseberry pie; loganberries, and red and black raspberries, two or three varieties of blackberries, and several kinds of grapes.

"For the hundreds of pounds of walnuts and filberts, a set of drying racks was constructed above the furnace. The trays had wire mesh bottoms so the heat could circulate around the nuts. Every so often Dad would crack a few so he and Mama could see how they were drying, and he stirred them up every day so they would dry evenly. As soon as he thought they were ready, he would take them down and put more up.

"Bartlett pears required special care to time the picking. When Dad thought they were about ready, he would carry several to the County Agent, where they were tested. When the test said it was time, we all got out and picked all the pears immediately. They are picked green, and they would ripen in the boxes stored in the barn. They usually ripened where they were crowded together in the bottom of the boxes, so it was a race to get them canned before they got too ripe." If Bartletts are allowed to ripen on the trees, they have a poor, grainy texture.

CHAPTER 40

Climate

Western Oregon climate is usually very mild, and weather-related crises, other than flooding, are rare; it  is known for its pretty steady rainfall through late Fall, winter, and early Spring. But one year, as Nancy remembers, when the leaves were still on the trees, we had colder than usual temperatures, below freezing—and it rained. "Ice formed on everything. Wires, tree branches and shrubs were covered. Icicles from the eaves of one-story houses in town reached to the ground. The whole of Western Oregon was like an ice palace. It was incredibly beautiful, but <u>devastating</u>. The electric and telephone lines became so heavy they sagged and then snapped. Huge branches and even whole trees, burdened with tons of ice, split and came crashing down. We tried to knock some of the ice off from the trees and wires, but new ice kept forming as it continued to rain. It was a sad year for the whole area, with power outages and many emergencies, and much loss of trees and shrubbery.

"Another year, we had an equally rare major snow storm. The snow was heavy and wet and nearly two feet deep.

Again, it was <u>so beautiful</u> but very hard to deal with. We don't have the facilities or equipment for much snow. This was later in the year, so the leaves were off the trees, and it was less damaging than the silver thaw had been, but caused inconvenience and hardship all over the Valley.

"This part of the country — all of the Pacific Northwest — had unusually heavy rains in 1941-1942. The floods were major; I was about seven, and the impressions are still vivid. This was the year the development at Vanport was wiped out by floods, and much of the Valley was in trouble. At the Farm, Mary's River was frequently over its banks, but this was more than that. The water began at the foot of the hill on which the house is standing, and stretched all the way to the riverbed. There were no fields, no fences; and part of the time, the roads were altogether impassable. The water was dark, muddy and swift. Every obstacle created swirls and eddies, and brown foam formed wherever there was even a slight drop. It was frightening. We lost power, of course, and used candles and lamps, and Mama cooked on the little wood trash burner stove and in the fireplace. Lots of rich topsoil was lost, and gullies and drainage ditches grew much larger, and some changed channels. There were other years of floods, but never so extreme again as that one. Jodie said that Dad told us not to worry—the Army Corps of Engineers would have the flooding contained some day."

CHAPTER **41**

The War Years

Ethel's journal: "Edward was in college before the war. He had spent the summer as a lifeguard on the river. He was in the ROTC, so had to leave for war training. He went into the Armored Division and served for a time. Then he transferred to the 82nd Airborne as a paratrooper and was sent overseas. He landed in Normandy and was with the **Screaming Eagles** at Bastogne that Christmas. One night, about midnight, I wakened — couldn't move — something was wrong. I wakened Ed. Later we received a letter from Edward — midnight was the moment he had landed in Normandy.

"We hung blankets at the windows for blackouts — the whole Pacific Coast was 'blacked out.' Whenever the *Star Spangled Banner* was played on the radio, all of us stood up, and it was often. Poor Grandad!" *(I missed my father when I came back home, but I was always glad that he didn't have this grief and worry. He passed on in 1938.)*

"When the war was over," Ethel wrote, "Edward came home, finished college, and was married to beautiful Jaclyn Flynn. Just before the service Edward asked Kent to <u>not</u> play with his little car during the ceremony — Kent always made the sounds of the motor — *brmmm! Brmmm!* After the wedding when Edward and Jacki boarded the plane and it left — I saw the lights way overhead in the dark sky —

leaving—my heart knew that it was the end of an era."

During the war, Jodie went up to Portland to take nurse's training. She loved it, but was not sufficiently prepared, she found. Jodie completed high school in three years, and she has written, "I really wish I had taken my senior year in high school instead of graduating early. I would have had chemistry and more math and would have been able to complete my nurse's training." She and Winston Majors were married in the front yard in May of 1946. I flew down from Everett, Washington, for the wedding. It was so pretty. The lilacs were in bloom, and the yard was filled with the fragrance of them. Dear Father Neville, such a friend of the family, performed the service. We had chairs set up, and Grandad was sitting in the front row, and right in the middle of the Lord's Prayer, asked loudly: "Has that young man been to college?" The little pump organ had been brought out, and the young man who sang *"Always"* in his sweet tenor voice had to start the second time because he began an octave too high. We served elegant little ice cream roses instead of having a big wedding cake. Fifteen minutes before the service was to start, I found Jodie in the upstairs bathroom washing her hair. She dried her pretty curls with a towel and put on a dainty wreath of tiny pink rosebuds and looked like an angel.

Nancy was her sister's attendant—her "maid of honor." She was thrilled. There were a good number of guests there, including Grandmother Wood, a friend dear to the family, who had paid for Ed's musical education when he was a boy. The yard was a perfect setting for a wedding. In 1938, Dot and Otto had also had their wedding there.

One summer I spent studying Oregon history (required for my teaching) at the Farm, and the whole family was wrapped up in it. I brought home every reference book on my correspondence list, and we shared all the excitement and color of that actually fairly recent time. I wanted so much to teach history and geography, but at that time it seemed that only the high school coaches were given those assignments, and my dean advised me to use the social studies as my minor, and major in business education. I did, and always had a job, but only a few times was able to teach my first love.

"When the Centennial was celebrated in Corvallis, Nancy was queen. Mama bought a bolt of black figured

calico-type material and made dresses for the girls and Lauri and me," says Jodie, "and shirts for Winston and Ralph, and matching doll dresses! She also bought a bolt of light blue print and made costumes for the seven Cordells (oh, we all had bonnets to match our dresses also). There was a costume contest and the folks didn't enter us (on purpose, because we have so much), and of course, Cordells won it. This is really good, but I wasn't so sure at the time. Another thing Dad didn't let me do. There was a milking contest, and he wouldn't let me enter because I'd have won it 'hands down' — those other girls wouldn't have had a chance! We were all in the parade, and it was a fun and exciting time. Dad and most of the other men grew beards — he looked really distinguished, much older, and we were all glad when it came off."

"When I graduated from high school," Nancy enjoys remembering, "the folks had a big yard party for the

graduates and their teachers. There were 150 in my graduating class, and over a hundred of them came. The food was excellent and it was such fun. I think some of the guests got a chance for a brief ride, but the number of horses was way down then — maybe only Chief — and he wasn't a horse to turn over to the inexperienced.

"For years, the Memorial Union staff held a big salmon bake at the Farm, every year. Duane (Dewey) Fitzgerald (Dad's MU Assistant) would come out and start a big log burning in the oak yard. There were huge fillets, half a salmon each, arranged on stakes along each side of it to cook, Indian style. Dewey seasoned the food with his own special blend of spices and condiments, and it was delectable. He would come out to tend the fish—turn it, move it to better spots, and so forth. This was during the MU planning conferences when they were laying out their year's agenda. No other salmon has ever had the flavor and juicy goodness of that salmon, eaten out under the trees, with everyone having such a wonderful time."

From Ethel's journal: "Kent took NROTC in college and received a Navy scholarship. He graduated in Political Science from the University of Washington, and he and Marlene Hankins were married there. After graduation, he served his three years in the Navy Air Force in Japan. He then went to Berkeley for graduate studies. He was also working for Homesmith Company in Mt. View. One day in 1959 he was returning home from work with his partner, and

was killed in a car accident, hit by car thieves who were fleeing from officers in hot pursuit. That day in October, I was picking up walnuts and suddenly felt surrounded by a thick fog. It frightened me and I went into the house. The telephone rang; Ed was there and answered, and was told about Kent's death. He hung up and we cried in each other's arms."

Such a sad time for our family. Norman and Lauri and I were back out in the Philippines that year, and when I read Dot's letter, my heart broke. Kent was beautiful, endearing, and so precious to us. Again, I felt so far away from my family and home.

Ethel registered for art classes at the University, keeping her hands and mind busy with new activities, helping to keep her mind off the tragedy. One of the striking art objects she created for the yard was a large white fish, on which rested a deep blue glass ball. I have a whole collection of little brown quail she made, and several lovely vases and jugs. One summer she took Lauri to class with her a few times, and Lauri learned to do some lovely things.

CHAPTER 42

Kent

Kent and Nancy were teenagers, and Kent kept us laughing in those days. Kent never came into the kitchen without dramatizing it—either prostrating his over six-foot body on the floor with mournful cries of "water! water!" or reaching into the dish cupboard through the one small window that didn't have a glass in it to get his tumbler, then having trouble getting it out.

He was not a natural athlete, but was quick and smart, and worked hard at his basketball, even achieving the high school team. His claim to fame, however, was the night he put the ball in the opposing team's basket, giving them the point. Total humiliation!

Kent was so beautiful, and we loved him so. His appetite was incredible, although he never seemed to gain an ounce. Tall, slim, with blonde curly hair, he seemed to have everything.

When he graduated from high school, Norman wanted to celebrate with him, so took him out for a milk shake. Kent had two hamburgers and two milkshakes, and I don't remember what else. Norman couldn't believe it. I have seen him get up from the table after a big meal and go right to the refrigerator. He always drank at least three glasses of milk at a meal. One snowy day I was going somewhere with my tiny baby, wrapped totally in her soft pink Kenwood blanket, and Kent cried, "Evelyn, you have the baby upside down!" I didn't, of course, but for a moment I was shocked!

This dear boy, who when he was twelve would recite the total dialog and action from every movie he saw, following you from room to room to tell it all, became a naval officer, and flew multi-engine fighter planes. He served his time in Japan and elsewhere, and came back home to begin his life. The tragic accident that took him from us was crushing to the whole family, but we love his memory. The work he was doing was so typical of his spirit. He and his friend and partner—they had grown up together—went into the business of service to anyone with a problem. They would tackle anything, calling in whatever expert help they needed, and they were doing well.

Part IV:

A NEW GENERATION

Four generations (clockwise from upper left):
Karen, Nancy, Ethel, and baby Rachel

CHAPTER **43**

Linden

Linden expresses the feelings of the next generation: "The lane up to Grammy's house is graveled, really just two ruts with a ridge of green growing up the middle. It winds its way to a small two-car garage set apart from the house. Over the garage is an apartment—we lived there when our house at Burnt Woods burned down. I remember having the first doll I ever loved in this apartment—it was given to me in a small trunk.

"Along the garage there is a breezeway to keep the rain off when you walk from the garage to the house. Before you reach the house there is a little stone house used as a pantry. It has shelves on four walls, and they contained what seemed to me a huge amount of canned goods, mostly food that Grammy had canned herself. Those shelves were always neat and orderly—this in my early years impressed me immensely!

"As you entered the house, the first room on the left contained a large wood furnace that heated the whole house. This room also contained coat racks, drying racks for nuts. Grampa Walker also kept his tools in the furnace room, for yard, garden, carpentry, mechanics, or whatever.

"Just past the furnace room was what we referred to as the school room, with six little old classroom desks. Each desk was labeled with numbers for math, cursive writing, printing—so as we children progressed we could advance to the next desk. There was also a chalkboard. Across from the school room was the guest room, which had been the sewing room. In this room I fondly remember a baby crib that had painted on it the name of every baby who had slept in it!

"Next is the kitchen. There's a lot to be said for kitchens—the warmth and good smells, but what I remember most is how Grammy would save toast for me, just the way I liked it, dry and crunchy. She had a special place in the cupboard for my toast. This made me feel special, and very much loved.

"Now just off the kitchen was a small room where Grampy would sit with his leg propped up to bring comfort to that old WWI wound. Grampy played a lot of cribbage while sitting there, and tried to teach me the game when I was small. He made the most horrendous noises as he cleared his throat and sinuses. I don't think he was aware of it, but those noises scared the daylights out of us kids!

"Next there was a laundry room, with cement sinks and a water saving device. There was a small door opening to little 'munchkin' stairs that led up to an attic room. There were trunks of old clothes, and we'd play dress-up there. We had a variety of clothes, like purple velvet and feathers—I can remember dressing up to be anything I could imagine. This little room is a cherished wonderful place in my childhood memories.

"Next to the dining room was the living room, with a piano, and a large fireplace you could walk around. And in the dining room there was another fireplace. Grammy had made a rug to fit that entire room, with her own hands.

"Upstairs was a huge bathroom, close by a wonderful greenhouse. Grampy and Grammy's bedroom had a huge four-post bed. Adjoining their room was an attic room with twin beds. When we kids stayed over, we'd usually sleep in that room.

"In Aunt Nancy's room was a large comfortable bed that I was allowed to sleep in after she went off to college. She also had beautiful figurines of old-fashioned ladies she had molded from clay.

"Near our play-house, behind the house, was our patio. It was made of rock; the little paths from the house to the playhouse were also rock. And there was a rock barbecue and a rock birdbath—all made by Grampy from the rocks that we kids had collected. Also the walls around the patio had pretty rocks in them, collected by the children.

"The path from the patio went down into Aunt Nancy's forest; we all believed she had planted it. The lower limbs were always trimmed back so people had room to walk around. It was bordered by a fence, to separate it from the big field, and there was a stile there to get over the fence. I remember crossing these steps when I was very young, and it seemed such a wondrous adventure to me.

"Up the path to higher ground on the other side of the house leads us to a big slide, made from an old school house fire escape. It was about twenty feet high, and more great fun for us. Once I took little Lauri Jo down it—I wasn't supposed to, but she enjoyed it!

"Not far from the slide I remember a hammock, and the trapeze I used to play on. I was the only one who used it. I could hang by my toes, and I certainly thought this to be a great accomplishment!"

CHAPTER 44

Lea

Lea shared with me pages of memories, beginning with "I smell sweet home-made bread. I remember walking into the kitchen and great beautiful loaves of bread were on the counter at my Grammy's. She always had slices of toast down in the beautiful hutch, and as a treat sometimes the toast would have a piece of cheese on it.

"I remember when I was about five running in so excited to show her that I could tie my own shoe laces. She stopped everything—this very busy lady, to watch while I tied my own shoes, and she was so excited with me!

"I remember the little upstairs room over the laundry, with the big wicker basket of dress-up clothes. They belonged to my aunts, and they were so tiny that when I was in the second grade their shoes fit my sisters and cousins and all of us. We had such a wonderful time—there were hats and heels, and long black dresses with dazzling sparkles on the shoulders.

"I remember the school room Grammy fixed for us. It had beautiful little blue desks painted with the ABC's on them. There was a chest of drawers with paper and pencils and color crayons, and there was a chalkboard and chalk. We loved playing school.

"I remember the big rope in the barn we used to swing on by the

hour. When I'm canning applesauce, even to this day, the aroma reminds me of the milking barn, because that was where the apples were always stored for the winter.

"One special summer evening when I was about ten my grandfather had gone on a trip and I was to be the one to go spend a night with my Grammy. We didn't live but a mile away. I was so excited—as I was walking I had a bag in one hand and my other hand was stuck straight out in front of me. Grammy was waiting at the end of the lane for me. I still can hear the big old grandfather clock ticking in the quiet of the night.

"I was always afraid to go into the dark fruit house. When they sent me to bring something out—pickles, or pears, or whatever—I always tried to have someone with me. It was so cold in there, even in the summer, and dark!

"The lunches at the Farm were so good! There was always something fun and different—home-made mayonnaise, of course; great big beautiful cookies for dessert, kept in a big brown jug. (I have that jug now.)

"I loved to be the one to take someone out there; I felt so proud, walking down the breezeway with the beautiful camellias on both sides, and grapes overhead. We used to pick the little sour things off the grapevines and suck them.

"And I can remember how I loved sitting by the fire in the kitchen picking out the nutmeats while Grammy cracked the nuts on the hearth with her pretty painted hammer. She painted anything she could get her hands on. She was always busy—I don't think I ever saw her just sit. I can see her always moving, putting scrapbooks together, planting flowers, painting doors, ceilings, cupboards, happy and never complaining.

"She let me comb her pure white hair, and I think she enjoyed it. She always wore it up in a French bun. She looked so different when it was down. Her hair was always so pretty.

"One of my favorite places was Grampy and Grammy's bedroom. I loved the huge bed my grandfather had especially made. Grammy had to step on a stool to get in.

Sometimes we spent a night in the attic room. I loved it, with its little window that pushed out so you could see — mostly I remember just the top of the house.

"There was a small greenhouse upstairs, too, by the bathroom. My Aunt Nancy grew pretty flowers in it. The bathroom smelled like Grammy, powdery and sweet.

"Christmas was a wonderful time. We always had so much food. We loved sitting on the big old brown couch, because we sank in so far. Everyone had something special to bring and Auntie Dot's plum pudding sticks in my mind the most.

"One time my sister Linden had her birthday there and my Uncle Kent was there. When I told him that my birthday had been just eight days before, he left the table and went up to his room. He brought down a pink paper parasol from Japan. I was elated — he was one of my favorite persons. One Christmas when he was home on leave, he was by the fireplace in the living room. Linden and Gay were in with me and they told him my deep dark secret — that I loved him and when I grew up I was going to marry him. I was so embarrassed I ran and hid.

"I remember picking the ripe peaches in the orchard and Grammy spooning the thickest cream and some sugar on top of a dish of them. It was so good.

"We had a lovely swing out in the yard. It was so big it felt as though you could almost touch the sky. When you were there you were in another world. I can also remember when I couldn't fit in the baby swing any more. That was a long time ago!

"We used to have cookies and tea in the playhouse, which is still there. We played by the hour down in the forest. It was our fairyland — a place for pretending.

"One year my Bluebird group went over and raked leaves for my Grammy to earn money for our group.

"Many different families stayed in the apartment over the garage. We stayed there once when our house at Burnt Woods burned down. I was about five. In later years, Aunt Edith lived there. She was deaf, but we always understood each other. She made the best biscuits and homemade chicken and noodles.

"I remember my piano lessons—reading stories—and love—All these things are a joy to remember in my life. The floors were always warm with all my grandmother's wonderful hooked rugs. When I look at the ones I have in my home now I can see her hands working away, creating always—it brings a smile and a little sadness. I'm grateful we all had the Farm for our haven for so long. I was able to have four of my six children there before it was sold. Dessa, my oldest, and Hank, played in the playhouse that all of us played in. We still feel that it's ours. Mr. Cornelius has given me many starts of Grammy's plants and roses.

"I remember the times playing with all the cousins. Once Clark, Lauri, Linden and I were bouncing on boards (I'm sure we weren't supposed to), and Clark got a nail in his bottom. Of course he was too embarrassed to cry. I wish I had the old slide.

These memories are mine and I am writing this with and for my sister Gay, now in heaven with Grammy.

Ethel, baby Amber, Jodie, and Gay

CHAPTER 45

Gay

Gay, Jodie's talented, spontaneous, lovely middle child, we also lost to a traffic accident. Driving into Corvallis one winter night, she hit ice on the little bridge near Wren, spun and rolled over, and was so injured that she survived only a few hours — not long enough for Jodie to get to her. It was like a light going out for all of us. Like Nancy, her talent for drawing and illustrating seemed to be just a part of her; she sang, rode horseback, loved and was beloved. The Philomath church was packed for her memorial service, and Ethel, who sat dazed through the service, decided it was wonderful to see all her friends and family, and went home without really accepting what had happened. Gay left two small sons, Shawn and Winston, and a teenage daughter, Amber.

CHAPTER 46

Lauri

L auri had her first visit to the Farm when she was ten days old. Norman brought me to Corvallis to have my baby here instead of in Bend, and the only hospital, fifty miles away. We were living in Gilchrist, I was teaching school and he was the Logging Superintendent. It was mid-winter, snow was deep, sidewalks treacherous, and the highway unpredictable. When it was just a month before the baby was due, I slipped and sat down hard on the icy sidewalk, and that was enough to convince Norman it was time to go to the lowlands. So the first of December found me warm and comfortable at the Farm, a perfect place to be, playing with 8-month-old Lea.

Lauri was born on December 29, and she and I stayed at the Farm for two weeks after we left the hospital. I don't

know who was having the most fun—I with my new baby, or Ethel with another precious one to rock. For the last month before Lauri was born, I had to teach Ethel how to drive my little car, since I could no longer get behind the wheel comfortably and still reach the clutch, and she had never driven anything but very large cars. She loved it. That month was fun, and we had a wonderful sister time, getting ready for Christmas, waiting for the baby. She was due Christmas Day, but waited sweetly until just after, so I could participate in all the marvelous festivities, and enjoy having everyone "take care" of me. Jodie already had Linden and Lea, only a year apart, beautiful chubby babies.

So now Lauri says, "Many miles away and many years later just the two words 'the Farm' evoke an overwhelming potpourri of memories and feelings. The Farm is so much more than a place in my past— it is my idyllic childhood (like Nancy), my familial strong spot, my dream of where I'd like to be later. The images are so rich and unending that trying to write about it is like trying to sort out the flavors of an Indian curry.

"The Farm is my link to a family I cherish. I am physically far from all of them, but close in heart to my aunts and uncles, my multitude of cousins, my grandparents, my precious parents, my beautiful daughters, and many friends and shirt-tail relatives. Our family tree looks more and more like a gnarled banyan, entwined with its own trunks and vines, sporting air roots and odd knots all over. But it stands rooted firmly, with one of those roots being the Farm.

"Most of my memories of the Farm are from my childhood in the 50s. During those years I was blessed with the close companionship of my five cousins, who lived variously at the Farm, next to the Farm, or close enough to be there often. My parents and I lived a few short hours away, and came for many weekends and during the summer.

"I remember long weeks in the summer when we came and stayed. Those were the times when my cousins and I didn't have enough hours in the days to do all the things available to us. We often started with a breakfast on the big cement patio, much to my father and Uncle Ed's discomfiture. They sometimes made their opinion expressively known by wearing mittens and scarves to our cool morning meal. I don't recall that their costumes had much effect on those early morning celebrations, other than to add a note of hilarity.

"The rest of those long summer days (always sunny and warm in my memory) were spent in extended fantasies that involved a variety of dress-ups. Auntie Ethel didn't just keep a box of old clothes for us to use. We had a whole room—the small attic up over the laundry room that was crammed with wonderful items for our adornment. Even cousin Ralph found enough masculine attire to properly transform himself. The dolls were up there too, and they were dressed up with us for our daily fantasy. Most of our dramas involved at least one queen and many princesses, thanks to marvelous old sheer curtains and several befitting tiaras. If we weren't queens and princesses, we were brides and bridegroom. The imbalance of five brides to one unwilling bridegroom was scarcely troubling in those days.

"As soon as the fashion of the day was decided upon, we spent the rest of the day roaming the Farm. We always had puppies or kittens to dote upon, and usually to dress up like dolls. We had a small playhouse to use for all kinds of imaginings, often mixing fantasies into a wonderful blend of brides and forts and long journeys. Lea had a melodramatic flair, so there was sure to be tragedy and adventure throughout our day.

"Our adventures often took us to the SLIDE, erected over the chicken house out of sheet metal. We spent many wonderful hours there. For a few of those years, there were chickens—hens and a rooster or two living below the slide. The chickens were not taken with six or more children noisily invading their space, so took the offensive when they saw us coming. This added to the adventure, as we had the 20-yard dash from gate to ladder before we were safe from the rooster's aggression. Burlap gunnysacks made the slide slicker, as did water. Our parents banned the use of water, since the Farm ran on a well, and we were perfectly capable of sliding until the well ran dry. But the sacks sufficed and we came down the slide at death-defying speeds in as many different postures as we dared. Once on the ground, more speed was needed to beat the rooster to the ladder. The summer that the chickens were given up as not profitable, the slide held less attraction for us. The fact that we were usually still garbed in long dresses with flowing veils, and often in high heels, made the slide even more of a challenge.

"Another activity we all enjoyed was in the barn. In my memory, we were usually in fairly normal play clothes for this endeavor, although I still see Lea wearing something fluttery. In the barn were two lofts that held much fascination for us. One loft was about two feet higher than the other. Between the two lofts hung the ROPE. The rope was absolutely the most challenging, scariest thing I did as a child. It never ceased to attract me. It never ceased to scare me to death. The rope was the firmest, most consistent lesson I had in answered prayer, because I never would swing over without first praying for safe journey.

"The trick was to swing from loft to loft on the rope. The journey from the high side to the low side was fun and without risk, if you dropped off in time. Since the higher side was so much higher, your feet wouldn't touch the low loft when you swung over, so you did have to drop a mere two feet or so. This was nothing for a herd of kids who regularly "bailed out" of swings.

"The fear and thrill came when we went from low to high side. If you stood at the very edge of the loft, reached as high on the rope as you possibly could, and swung your legs as far up as possible when you got to the other side, you had a fair chance of making the high loft without banging your body against the side of it. If you misjudged, you had two options—swing on the rope back to the lower side, hoping you had enough power to get all the way back; or let the rope swing back and forth in the middle until you got enough courage to drop to the ground, about 30 feet below.

"Sometimes we devised elegant rescues for the person dangling in the middle, capturing the rope with a stick and bringing it to the low side. Sometimes hay was hurriedly piled up on the ground below and the hapless hanger was encouraged to drop. I had done all of it: succeeded, swung back to the low side, slammed my body against the loft, been rescued, and dropped to what I thought was death. Through it all I never was seriously hurt, but there were a few broken arms on less experienced relatives and acquaintances.

"As I look back, I can't believe the adults in the crowd let us explore those lofts and ride that rope. The only explanation that comes to my mind is that they simply didn't know how hard it was to do. The barn was an elegant, rich-smelling playground for us. For the adults it was a place for hard work and messy cows. *(Note from Lauri's mother: I almost fainted when I read this the first time. Lauri was a small-boned child, my little girl. Hah. I had no idea that she was engaged in anything like this, or the slide, or bailing out of the big swing. I'm sure that we were both happier that I didn't know!)*

"One of the lofts held trunks of old, honestly antique clothes. We were behooved not to play with those clothes, and we really didn't. Sometimes, with permission, we looked through them and put on the hats, but there was a thick line between those trunks and the dress-ups we loved so well. Later those clothes went to a museum, sadly behind glass where no little hands can feel the smoothness of the satin and the stiffness of the lace.

"Bales of hay were stored in one of those lofts. We climbed precarious mountains and hid behind prickly, dark piles in endless games of reality and fantasy. I remember the rules—practical and few—don't break open the bales and don't try to move them. Moving even one bale could cause a whole stack to shift dangerously. In my memory, we did follow those rules unless we needed loose hay for one of our daring rescues.

"There was more to the Farm than just the barn and the dress-up room. To the front and side of the house was a small stand of fir and pines. By the time I was roaming the area, the trees were six to eight feet tall. The "forest" was cool and damp, not big enough to get lost in, but big enough to escape to. We certainly played down there. But the forest was also my first experience in being peaceful and away from everybody by choice. I often took a book to read or just a kitten for company, and wandered down. The floor was clear of underbrush, and there were no fallen logs in such a young area. There were some big stones and a few stumps for sitting. It was sweet, green, quiet, and inspirational. It was safe, even for a young, not very brave little girl. When the chosen kitten squirmed away or the book lay forgotten, when someone called for dinner, or the need for solitude passed, the familiar and busy house was a short sprint up a stone path into a regular lawn. Little did I then realize what a treasure it was to have a forest at your bidding. What a shock when I returned to the Farm 30 years later — the trees were so tall. But the call to wander in was still there and the forest remains a treasure on the property.

"The whole family gravitated to The Farm for the important events of life. Engagement announcements, weddings, graduation, new babies, Christmases, memorial services, visiting relatives, and reunions attracted us like magnets. Other times lured us there — apple, peach, and pear-picking times, college football and basketball games, and just wonderful summer vacations. When I was ten we moved to the Farm for awhile. Even though I lived there for short periods of time off and on for several years, and lived close by for years, it never lost the magic.

"When we lived there, my bedroom (formerly Jodie's, then Nancy's) was off the master bedroom, upstairs. Some tree branches rubbed the house at the slightest breeze. My imagination and timidity made that a rather frightening time for me, but I learned my multiplication tables perfectly by reciting them every night until I could finally drop off to sleep. Years afterwards my mother asked me why I hadn't mentioned the disturbing noise to anyone. It never occurred to me that the problem could be fixed."

Jodie certainly had the same problem when she was a little girl and occupied that bedroom She added, "There were those who would have called the big old neglected house 'haunted.' It did look that way when we first moved in, but I never had that feeling about it. There were times and incidents, though, that seemed spooky. The old house creaked and groaned when it cooled off at night, and seemed to move when the wind blew strongly; mice and squirrels rattled nuts across the attic, shadows moved mysteriously, the moon peeking in the window created figures on the wall, and always there was the rubbing of the branches. Sometimes if I were alone at night and the wind was blowing I'd hide under my covers. It sounded as though someone were coming up the stairs! — but of course I knew there wasn't anyone.

"Once, while Kent was a baby and in the crib with the screens on the sides and the big wheels, in Mama's room, I was supposed to be sleeping, but I didn't want to, because the family was having a party downstairs. The wind was blowing and the moon was bright, and as I peeked out from under the covers, the trees were making moving patterns on the side of the crib. The more I watched the uneasier I got until I couldn't stand it any longer. I thought I saw a face! I tiptoed shakily toward the stairs, never taking my eyes off the 'face' on the side of the crib. As I came close to the door and almost past the crib Kent let out a howl that would have raised the dead. I don't know how I got to the stairs, but everyone said I didn't touch a step all the way down—my nightgown flying out behind me. Dad had to go up with me and check it all out before I'd go back to bed. For the rest of her life, Mama would laugh about that little episode until she had tears in her eyes.

"Another time I remember particularly was when I was using Edward's room. The wind was whipping the trees and the house was creaking and something wakened me, and suddenly from their bedroom, Dad's mighty snore was really bad and it ended with a great snort. No one else was awake and I thought I'd been attacked by something unearthly! I wanted to waken someone else for comfort, but of course I didn't." Neither Lauri nor Jodie ever actually confided their fears until they were grown. As Lauri says, they didn't realize some of the problems, like the scratchy branches, could be easily fixed. What amazes me is that through all the years, and all the little occupants of that room, no one cut off those troublesome branches, or covered those eerie windows. Frightened children look everywhere, and our girls spent some harrowing moments.

Lauri says, "Auntie Ethel and Uncle Ed inhabited the master bedroom. The closet in their room formed a narrow hallway that led to a tiny, under-the-eaves bedroom. That room held a treasure that even we naïve children recognized as priceless. In the bookshelves and in baskets were stacks and stacks of old comic books. *Little Dot, Richie Rich, Superman*, and countless others were read over and over. It was almost like forbidden fruit for me, who had never owned a comic book in my life. These were originals, dating back to the early 40s, at least. There were even the 'Classic Comics,' with *Tom Sawyer, Journey to the Center of the Earth, Paul Revere*, and so many others spread out in colorful images. There were two little beds in the room, covered in old-fashioned quilts. Mostly you couldn't stand up straight, because each side of the ceiling sloped with the eaves. But standing was never an issue, as all <u>six</u> of us could peacefully fit on those beds and spend hours lost in a wondrous daze. Later that bedroom was reserved for any teenage boys who might be visiting, and there were several who practically had to be dragged out for other activities.

"My parents, when they were there, occupied the big bedroom which was known as Kent's room, having been my cousin Kent's growing-up space. The treasure in <u>this</u> room was a collection of *LIFE* magazines, dating back to the very first issue. They were a treasure trove of history. Little did I know that I was using 'original sources' when I did a report on Eva Peron using the articles I found in old *LIFE* stories. I don't know what happened to the collection, but I hope someone is storing them in a sunny, upstairs bedroom.

"The second floor bathroom was a gathering place. It was as large as a bedroom, lined with counters and cabinets. The old bathtub was the prime source of cleanliness in the house, although there was a shower downstairs. The tub was the source of anguish for the women of the house, since it never would give up the rusty stains from old pipes and hard well water. Much 'elbow grease,' bleach and cleanser were expended, to no avail—the orange ring remained.

"Next to the stool were two rugs in the shape of large feet. As a very sheltered and proper young lady, I never could figure out why those feet were always turned the wrong way around. I usually pointed them out as I sat there and contemplated the beautiful view over the fields that an entire wall of windows offered. The bathroom was warm, sociable, pretty, and anything but private.

"Nancy's greenhouse was built out over the roof, just off that upstairs bathroom. A quick step inside assaulted the senses with exotic odors, warmth and humidity, and all the colors of nature that could be found. Here she raised orchids, African violets, Hawaiian teardrops, and other exotics. It was a tiny room, probably no more than six by eight feet. When Nancy was no longer at home, I have no memory of the greenhouse, so it probably stood idle as a reminder of the one who has done so many interesting things and created such beauty as she has gone her way.

"The main floor of the house was a wonder of large rooms full of antiques and family treasures. The kitchen seemed the most important room, and it was huge. It was old-fashioned, with no built-in cabinets. The sink, stove, and hutch were bound in by add-ons. Auntie Ethel had released her artistic energies on every square inch of cabinetry with tole paintings that reflected stories and nature. Off to the side was an eating area, an enormous refrigerator, and the keeping room, where there was a big fireplace around which the family gathered. For some years there was a couch, a great chair for Uncle Ed, various perching spots, and a handy table for numerous games of cribbage between the men. I never really learned the game, but I can clearly hear my Dad and Uncle Ed keeping score, '15-4, 15-6, 15-8..."

"In much later years a television also resided in this cozy area. No matter what family event was happening, the men gathered here, surrounded by various children and older aunties and grandmas. The women buzzed happily in the main part of the kitchen and the repartee between the two areas never ceased.

"Another big room was the dining room. I would call it a 'formal' dining room, with china cabinets and a huge table, but the gatherings here were anything but formal. I joyously remember vast birthday parties with home decorated cakes; and great family meals—breakfasts, lunches, dinners, and sumptuous desserts.

"I also remember projects: cutting things up, making scrap books, wrapping presents, learning to make Christmas ornaments. The window of my memory lets me see my youngest cousin, Peggy, being nursed in one quiet corner

while the family carried on. It spans years and jumps to almost the final days at the Farm, holding Lea's baby while my own grew big inside me.

"My wedding reception was held in this room, amidst the dearest of family and friends. Mom was teaching high school, and had recruited two of her students—identical twin sisters—to serve.

"The funny family tales that grew to legend in that room reflect the humor and love that was in abundance. The day my darling carousel birthday cake went up in flames because the paper top caught on fire from the candles brings giggles to Mom and me even now. The table itself gave shelter to many children who slid out of chairs when the conversation grew too long for them.

"Wandering from the dining room with full tummies and stimulated minds, we gathered in our biggest crowds in the living room. This was the least-used room downstairs, but surely one of the most interesting. A great fireplace stood in the center of the room, not on a wall, but dividing the room. Back of the fireplace was a little black piano, a pump organ, shelves of books, and quiet little chairs that invited perching. In front, there were two large couches, the Bouden piano, and some grandmother rockers. It was in this living room that we held the most cherished of all family gatherings—Christmas.

"Christmas began early in the morning with the ingathering of relatives from Portland and Salem. Aunts and grandmothers who didn't drive arrived from all points, picked up by other sets of relatives who did drive and were also coming. The cousins arrived *en masse*. In the kitchen there was hustling about as the Christmas breakfast was being assembled. Uncle Ed would be making his amazing cereal—so full of dates, raisins, nuts and all good things it was honestly a real treat to eat. Fresh fruits, sweet rolls (Auntie Dot's *stollen*), piles of toast, plates of bacon and sausage, a pitcher or of orange juice, and always the smell of fresh ground and brewed coffee made breakfast a feast.

"But breakfast for kids on Christmas was a real bother, because the tree could not even be touched until breakfast, with chatty adults, was not only eaten, but cleaned up! I can still feel the sense of impatience that permeated our mood on those mornings. After all the relatives were accounted for, the presents all piled under the tree, the breakfast eaten, the kitchen polished and ready for another go-round, the roasting turkey duly admired by all the aunts and grandmothers, and everyone seated comfortably near the tree — then began the opening of the presents.

"In those days we all gave presents to everyone. We were not wealthy, although I didn't know that, but the presents we gave were magnificent gifts from the heart. My allowance stretched and stretched as I looked for a pretty hanky for Aunt Grace or decorated a jar of homemade jam for Nanny. The uncles taxed my imagination, so they were often the recipients of a special bag of nuts or some unique  gadget I was sure they needed. Every child received gifts from all of the adults in the exact same spirit. Many of the gifts were handmade — my aunts and uncles were all talented and resourceful. One year Uncle Otto gave each family a delightful birdfeeder on a post, carved by hand. We cousins always received new warm nightgowns from Auntie Ethel, made of soft, pretty flannel. Usually there was one new outfit for each child, sometimes homemade, sometimes store bought. Games, dolls, books, and toys were in abundance. With five cousins in one family, and me, I'm sure it taxed their ingenuity to keep it as even as possible.

"Joke presents always popped up. Dad and Auntie Ethel exchanged the same pair of socks year after year. That began after he had teasingly 'helped' her darn the heels. Since that rendered them totally unusable, they began appearing at Christmas, with new additions each time. Once there were buttons sewn on them. Another year they acquired odd-looking scraps of material on the outside. One year the ladies in the family had requested autographed photos of Ava Gardner, and gave them with personal message to each of the men.

"The dinner, early in the afternoon, found us gathered back in the dining room. Sometimes the children had separate tables, when there were too many of us. Turkey, ham, sweet potatoes, cranberry sauce, vegetables, fruits, and wonderful desserts — my memories don't center on any one food — just a feeling of lots of smells, tastes, sounds, and people. Everything in my memory glows warm and bright. After dinner, the men took the youngest children for walks and the older children were pressed into service to help wash and dry endless stacks of dishes. (There never was an automatic dishwasher in that house.) The kitchen was a beehive of activity as all the aunts, grandmothers, and teens did their best to make the kitchen return to normal. I can hear my Auntie Mary's infectious laugh even now. She always had a dozen stories to tell, a rapid-fire delivery, and a quickness in her movements that made her seem like the center of a large whirlpool.

"The mood of the day continued, swirling around tired children and dozing uncles. The women found quiet nooks to chat about their families. Sometimes a group gathered at the piano to sing carols, with Uncle Windy playing. Sometimes a brave aunt (and once my mother) bundled all the cousins up to go to the movie in town. We filled a whole row at the Majestic Theater!

"When daylight waned, uncles and aunts, grandmas and cousins prepared to take their leave. Giant bear hugs from Uncle Windy, sweet-smelling kisses from grandmas, last minute whispers from cousins gradually brought the day to a quiet end. As I tried to recreate family Christmas for my own children in later years, I was aware of the treasures I lacked — an old farmhouse, an abundance of relatives, and the innocence of a time gone by.

"I remember the last Christmas we spent at the Farm. My daughter Jennifer was growing within me. Lea had two little ones already. The grandmothers were gone, the mothers were grandmothers, and the cousins were parents. The uncles were gone, too, except for my Dad. There were new faces—spouses, babies, and friends. Auntie Ethel was going to move to town and the Farm would be sold—out of the family. It was unthinkable, and so we didn't think about it. I held Lea's littlest one and dreamt of bringing my own children to the Farm.

"The breakfast was delicious, although no one even thought of serving cereal. The gifts were given out, and there was an abundance of homemade beauty to be treasured. No one dressed up—no one modeled new outfits or warm pajamas. I don't remember all of the day, but I can see the faces. Lea—so beautiful as a young mother with equally beautiful children; Auntie Ethel, radiant and serene even though she had tough decisions to make and a new life to prepare for; Mom, assuming the role of the matriarch even then, coordinating the kitchen with young adult women ready to do the work.

"There was plenty of laughter in the kitchen, plenty of conversation between watchers and workers. Dad was the only older man. There were new young men, but none of them played cribbage. Still the warmth of family and the day swirled around us, giving us one more Christmas to hold in our hearts."

CHAPTER 47

Second Visit

Two other times we lived at the Farm. First, only Lauri, who was eleven, and I, when Norman went back to the Philippine Islands ahead of us. Lauri was in school, and I did some volunteer work with her class. This was an anxious time for me, but Lauri and I loved being there. She was in the midst of her cousins, which always made it a special experience. After just a few months we joined Norman, I with an aching heart, not wanting to go there again, but hoping and praying for a good unfolding for our lives. While we lived out there, great tragedy struck when Kent was killed in an accident, and I was more ready than ever to get back home. And we did return in March, having asked for a release from Norman's contract.

We came back to the Farm. Once again, Norman was job-hunting, helping around the Farm, and I was attending the university to finally get my teaching certificate. Lauri was also back in school, so this was a busy time, and it was not long before we found a little home of our own. But each time, the Farm had been such a *haven* for us, so my memories, like those of the children, are deep and sweet.

Ethel wrote, "Nancy and Bob Ewalt were married in the Memorial Union lounge. It was a sweet wedding. She had made her dress, and Jodie's. They were married on Lauri's ninth birthday, December 29, 1957. Ed and Jodie accompanied Nancy down the aisle, and Father Neville performed the ceremony. Then Bob was in the Air Force and was stationed in Florida, where they had their first child, Mark. When Nancy was again expecting, in Illinois this time, I went to help her, taking Linden with me for company, and we stayed until after Katherine was born.

CHAPTER 48

Peggy ~ "Little Peg"

Little Peggy, Jodie's youngest daughter, wrote a composition one time for school. She called it, "The After School Swim." It wasn't long, but it paints a delightful picture: "We rode down to the river and swam after school. First we got all through with our chores, ate dinner, and  changed our clothes. After all this we caught the horses and proceeded to go to the river. Well we finally got down there and we were body surfing in some rapids and running, or trying to run through them. Finally we got tired and rode home." Peg and her friends Connie Wise and Erin Rycraft, used to dive the horses into the river and swim on them. The horses seemed to love it, too.

Peg also recalls, "I remember being wakened by a loud noise—it was the sound of snow sliding from the roof in the middle of the night. In the morning I could see the huge snowdrifts that had piled around the house from the roof—it had the look of a **no-school day** to me! Connie would be over in no time. After Gram fixed breakfast for Edith and me, we had many phone calls from friends asking if we needed anything —help—or whatever.

"Then the girls came—Cindy and Patty Parnell, and of course Connie. They all came to the Farm to share in the fun.

We all had horses there, you know. Connie had Shawna, Cindy's was Cinnamon, Patty rode Gypsy, and I had Lacy.

"On this special day we decided to pick on one horse, Gypsy. She wasn't very big, but she didn't need to be for what we had planned. We saddled her up and one of us held her while another of us ran to the tool shed and grabbed the sled. We tied a rope to the sled and made a loop around the saddle horn, then ran her up and down the long driveway, each of us having a sled ride, until Gypsy was worn out.

"After taking care of Gypsy we all went into the furnace room to shed snow clothes and boots. Gram always had a nice fire in the fireplace, and we had hot chocolate and butteered toast."

Another time, when the snow was deep enough and stayed long enough to be great for playing, Peggy and Connie joyously created  *Fresca*. They rolled giant balls of snow, and made a beautiful pony-sized horse. They saddled and bridled it, and provided a rider—Daisy, Peg's tiny toy white poodle. The weather stayed cold, so *Fresca* survived for a while almost intact. He did have a tendency to lose his head, but they quickly restored it. Peg says, "Gram loved it."

"The time I spent at the Farm seems much like a dream," notes Peg. "I went to live there not long after I turned thirteen. I had spent the previous summer on the Farm. It was a beautiful summer—Gypsy and I had long rides—I was able to have her there with me all summer. In the late afternoons, Gram, Grampy, Hans, and I would sit on the fish pool patio and have fresh peaches with sugar and cream, or cantaloupe with vanilla ice cream. Grampy would be on the chaise lounge resting while Gram would read to us. Hans was the black and tan dachshund that my mom had given them when he was just a puppy.

"Grampy died that summer, in June, and I went to live with Gram. It was late summer, and she had been traveling around Oregon and California with my Uncle Edward and Aunt Janet. And soon after that Aunt Edith came to live with us, too. She moved into the garage apartment. I was always amazed at her. I don't know how old she was then; she was deaf and her eyesight was not good, but she could chop wood — to this day I can't chop wood like that. She made the most wonderful pumpkin pies. Aunt Edith was the most selfless person I have ever met.

"On my sixteenth birthday I had a bunch of girls over to ride and play. Julie Gast's father brought her over, and she had a very tiny baby lamb for me. I was surprised that Gram let me keep him. We had to keep him in the furnace room until he was big enough to stay in the barn. He ran loose in the yard most of the time. We named him Hobo because Julie had found him in the hills where there were no other sheep.

When Hobo got big we had to lock him in the pasture with the horses, and he started to think he was a horse. He missed being able to run around in the yard, though, and would always find a hole in the fence as a way to get in. He would come to Aunt Edith's door and eat her flowers, and she would come out swinging a broom and yelling at him to run him off."

Little Peg as Maid Marion in the Philomath Frolic

CHAPTER 49

Katherine

Katherine Ewalt, one of Nancy's gifted children, and big sister to Karen and Kent, but second to Mark, has poignant and funny memories about her early childhood stays at the Farm. While they were living at Pullman, Washington, the children were often visitors. After their move to Texas, it was much farther, but still the magic was there and the pull always strong.

Katherine writes: "In the large upstairs bathroom of the Farm house, every morning Grammy would be the first one up, bathing and preparing for the day. When she had completed most of her routine, she would then open the door for the grandchildren to take their turns. I would sit on the toilet and watch her as she brushed her long white-with-silver streaked curly hair and wish that some day my hair would be so pretty — white, curly and long (that is why today I cannot complain with every new streak of gray hair that I see when I look in the mirror).

"She would be sitting in a chair, in front of a broad vanity table, facing a large mirror framed on either side by windows that looked out over the back yard and on to the wheat field which was bordered on two sides by the horse pasture, and on the third side by a grove of trees. This was a beautiful view of tall green trees, a garden, and just below, the back courtyard. I had never seen anyone use the courtyard, which was then grown up with Montana clematis, and usually covered with fallen leaves.

"As a little girl I sat on the toilet quietly each morning of every visit of every year. After watching Grammy, after looking out the window, and daydreaming, I would gaze at all the familiar parts of that large bathroom. The bathtub, without a shower, the pictures on the walls, the tole paintings here and there, rugs on the floor, and the special hooked rug with braided edging with the mare and foal resting under a tree — I knew them by heart.

"And looking down I would notice the feet. They were extremely large right and left feet, off white with pinkish edging, rugs that had been hand-hooked by Grammy — but they were always facing the toilet, backward! Each time when I finished I would have to turn those feet around so that they would be facing the right direction!

"Several years passed when I overheard my mother and Aunt Jodie discussing the feet. Apparently, Grampy had in earlier times complained of cold feet in the bathroom; so Grammy therefore had hooked the rug feet especially for him. A bell soon went off in my little head and I finally realized the feet had always been facing the correct direction, after all. Little girls are natural busybodies, and I had made it my business through the year to fix those feet! How Grampy must have chuckled!"

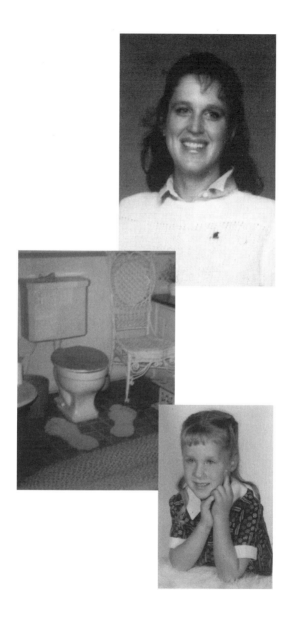

Part V:

THE END OF AN ERA

CHAPTER 50

Tomorrow

As the children and their children all grew up and left the Farm, there was a hiatus, when Ethel and Ed felt they were near the rainbow's end. She wrote in her journal:

"Then Ed and I were alone on the Farm, and Ed was quite frail — too frail to go to Oregon State's triumphant Rose Bowl game. So we went to Meier & Frank's in Portland and bought our first television set, an RCA, and put it into our kitchen family room. I drove home on the freeway, and an officer stopped me to see if there was something wrong — I was driving too slowly!

"A few short years later our dear Dr. Nick Tartar said that Ed must go to the hospital, so in June, 1966, he was taken by ambulance to the Veteran's Hospital in Portland. Nick took me to stay with Dot and Otto. Every day they brought me to the hospital to spend the day with Ed. On June 24th, when I told him goodnight, I said, 'I'll see you tomorrow.' He answered 'Tomorrow?' as though asking a question. At about two in the morning Dot wakened me for a telephone call. My precious Ed had gone to sleep forever. Part of me went with him."

In the last years, after Ed was gone, and Ethel and Edith and Ethel's beloved granddaughter Peg were living there, they were hiring help and struggling to keep the Farm as wonderful as ever. My heartstrings were tugged and my visits became more and more frequent. In her inimitable manner, Ethel still welcomed all who came to her door with warmth and generosity. There were still Camp Fire Girls and Mr. Hall's history classes, still cookies and hot chocolate, still fruit and flowers and her lovely welcoming smile. But there was such sadness, and her sense of loss was so great, that after eight years she consented to sell the Farm and move to a sweet home close to us, bringing Edith and their two little dachshund dogs and maybe a tenth of her treasures.

CHAPTER 51

Deciding to Move

Nancy says, "In 1972, Mama called me to visit. Little Peg was eighteen and about to leave. The house needed painting, and there were some plumbing problems. Some of the fences were down. It was almost impossible to get reliable help. Mama was thinking about selling the Farm. This was the first of many discussions we had over the next months about her feelings, fears, regrets, and loneliness. She urged everyone to be present at Christmas. Nearly all came. She announced that the Farm had been sold.

"We had all been so centered in The Farm that there was much shock, disbelief, desire to fix the situation—but it was done. There had been no one in the family to take it over, and it was much too much for her. With that, Evelyn and Norman helped her buy and fix up a nice little house on the street where they lived.

"In August of 1973, Bob and I and the children drove to Corvallis from Pullman, Washington, where we had been living. The van was loaded with our belongings headed for Lubbock, Texas, and our new job. We helped Mama see that her things for her new house were loaded into the moving van at the Farm. Our van had been there earlier to pick up furniture she had given us. Everyone in the family shared in the treasures; some were given to friends, and a few were sold. It was the end of a precious, unforgettable time for our whole family."

Ethel cherished Edith and was grateful for her companionship. She wrote, "Cecil Metcalf, Edith's husband, died about the same time as Ed, and Edith came to live in the apartment. We both felt lost, but there we lived for eight years. Jodie's Peggy came to live with me when she was 13, and was there until she was 18. Then I decided that it was time to make a change. Edith and I talked it over and made our decision together. There was a little house on Van Buren Avenue, very near Evelyn and Norman's, on the market. I sold the Farm to Grant and Gail Cornelius; gave and sold much of the furniture and many of the rugs, and moved, with the help of Bob and Nancy, Evelyn and Norman, Ginny Held, and other members of the family, into our little new home together — closing the book on the most precious home place."

The Farm went to new owners, the Corneliuses, fine and good people who cherish it and have done many wonderful things to it, and who warmly welcome us when we can visit there a bit. Ethel, Jodie, Lea and Peggy could never bring themselves to go back — it was just too poignant. But in 1995 I took Jodie, Nancy, Lea, Lauri, and my granddaughter Kimberly out to see how beautifully it had been kept, on the day of Ethel's memorial service. They loved seeing how much it remained the same — many paintings preserved in the house — the playhouse still standing, the forest and the Cecil Bruner rose still there. Lauri and Lea roamed and reminisced, and my Kimberly said to me, standing in the little forest, "Oh Grammy, this is an enchanted Farm.

CHAPTER 52

Cornelius

I asked Gail and Grant to add to our story, so Gail wrote, "In the early 1970's, we owned and operated a business in downtown Corvallis, The Inkwell. One evening Grant did not come home at the usual hour, and my repeated calls to the store brought no answer. When he finally arrived home I asked where he had been, and he said that on his way to the post office he had stopped to visit with Pat Stopp, a local realtor. The pressure of a late family dinner prohibited any more discussion about that visit just then.

"After church the following Sunday, Grant said he wanted to drive out south of town to see the 'Allworth estate.' Pat Stopp told him it might be coming on the market soon. I said, 'Estate! When a realtor calls a property an estate that just means you pay a higher price.' I wasn't interested

in moving at that time, and was sure I wasn't interested in an estate. However, as we drove slowly up the tree-lined lane and discovered the house nestled serenely under towering trees and overlooking extensive lawns, my attitude changed. We were both filled with a desire to see more.

"Monday we called Pat and asked to see the Allworth property when it came on the market. A few days later I received a phone call from Mrs. Allworth asking if we had ever had a tour of her home, and inviting us out to see it. On a very chilly, windy evening she walked the rounds with us, and showed us the house, fascinating us with an historical commentary of their years on the Farm. I fell in love with the big old house and Grant with the surrounding gardens. We both fell in love with Mrs. Allworth.

"We immediately submitted an offer. The ad that Pat Stopp had run in the *Gazette Times*, well-written and describing the Farm in glowing detail, had our 12-year-old son fuming that we might lose it. We felt the price was too high, but Pat told us that after the last couple she had taken out there was about to leave, Mrs. Allworth caught her eye and cautiously shook her head "no." Pat suggested we make another offer. We did, and were delighted to have it accepted. In August of 1973, we moved to the Farm.

"Grant had warned me that when Mrs. Allworth moved out, a lot of the charm of the house would go with her. It did—and still her footprints were everywhere. From the hooked rug on the stairs to the hand-painted scenes on walls, ceiling and woodwork, her talents beguiled us. We still have the tile-like painted ceiling in the family room, She told us she had to keep her hands and mind busy as she worried about her sister and brother-in-law who were in a Japanese prisoner of war camp in the Philippines, and her son who was in the war in Europe.

"The fireplace screens she painted remain in place. Angels and children continue to adorn the back of the corner cupboard doors in the dining room, and Baby Jesus still decorates the front entry door. Most precious of all, the hooked rug depicting the history of the United States still marches forthrightly up the stairs, creating wonderment in all who see it.

"A few years ago our son Eric and his wife Lisa restored the apartment originally built around 1945 over the garage. We call it 'the cottage.' The large mural Mrs. Allworth and Nancy had painted over the stove on the wall of the kitchen in the big house now hangs on a wall made just for it in the cottage. Eric, Lisa, and their little Chelsea and Maggie now live in the cottage.

"Over the years we have been guided by a strong desire to be good stewards and to maintain the historical integrity of the house and farm, yet wanting to make changes to suit our interests. In the 26 years we have lived here, both minor and major changes have occurred. Of the two major ones, only one was intended. In 1985, the barn burned down. An enormous structure with post and beam construction, it brooded over the entry courtyard. We loved that old barn and mourned its loss as one would for a member of the family. In the well-fertilized soil where the barn once stood, Grant now raises many varieties of berries and flowers.

"The other major change is the addition of a sunroom on the east side of the house, with access from the dining room and the family room. The design of the sunroom is such that it blends well with the old house, maintaining the integrity of the major structure. The location of the sunroom enables us to more fully enjoy the gardens on both the east and north side of the house. It is particularly delightful to watch the sun bursting over the horizon on a summer morning, creating a cathedral effect in the forest with an intriguing combination of light and shadow. On a clear day when the mountains come out of hiding we treasure the view of the snow-covered peaks.

"Perhaps I should include a third major change: extensive development of the grounds into gardens. Grant has long had a love of landscape gardening, and has done a sweeping renovation and development of the garden, which he now refers to as 'Century House Gardens.' Building on the well-planned, well-tended gardens that Mrs. Allworth left us, he has at least tripled the number of planting beds and added meandering paths where one can wander or sit and enjoy the beauty. We have hosted several garden tours for the public as fundraisers for various organizations. We never tire of the compliments expressed by our many visitors who share with us their gratitude for the opportunity to enjoy the beauty, peace, and solitude we have loved these many years. We believe those attributes are as strong today as when we were first attracted to them twenty-six years ago.

"Mrs. Allworth told us that at one time she had considered giving the Farm to the University. We are so glad that did not happen. This old house is so much more than a cold museum — it's the focal point of a vibrant, living history. Filled with character and charm, it is aging gracefully and will surely nurture loving families for many years to come. Yes, we do believe the Farm is an estate and more. No price could be high enough for us to let it go."

Epilogue

After he had paid off the Farm, Ed purchased the Alnutt place, and that lovely farm took a very high place in the family's affections, too. It is a beautiful piece of land, with an oak grove on a hilltop, and sweet little "woods" of oak where we knew there were deer, fox, and other little animals; and two beautiful fields under cultivation. There is also another marvelous old house, with a curving staircase, 25 great locust trees, and no heat but a wood stove. Norman and Lauri and I, and Edna, Norman's mother, lived there a few years, loving it, and feeling such a part of the Farm itself.

But we were never farmers. They are a special kind of people, close to the earth, economical about every resource, willing to be inconvenienced and overworked, acknowledging a kinship with the animals they raise and nurture and use. They understand the weather, the earth, the water, and animals. They have little time for entertainment or traveling, and they are not interested in "moving on." My sister worked as hard as any pioneer woman of the 19th century. She mended and re-mended, and taught her girls to do this. She was elegant and beautifully dressed when they socialized, but her usual attire was a housedress. She surrounded herself with beauty, but most of it was her own making.

My brother-in-law kept his university job until the traditional retirement age, but always kept up his share of the Farm work, even when he was quite crippled with arthritis. He simply loved to farm. His sons did not, but his daughters inherited that love, and both are still their happiest when they are in the country, working with their animals, doing what their parents did.

Nancy owns a small horse homestead in Texas, and has horses and chickens, goats and gardens, and does almost all of her own work, even building fences and operating the tractor. Jodie has always raised blooded horses and miniature horses in Eastern Washington, and registered toy poodles to sell. She has done a man's work until the last very few years on her small ranch. Jodie's daughter Peggy fits into the family mold, as does Nancy's Katharine in Texas. Peggy has a delightful small farm in the Willamette Valley, and has horses. Lea earns her living catering, but keeps chickens, rabbits, doves — anything else that comes along, right at the edge of Corvallis. These are all beautiful and strong women, in the mold of the Farm. The rest of us were just visitors to this farm life, privileged and happy, but not of the same fabric.

There's a magnetic quality to that life that pulls one in, but it's a hard life, and it isn't always pretty. I have never killed unwanted kittens from a too prolific litter, helped a cow in labor, cleaned out a barn, nor washed an udder. Those little tasks are without charm for me, and I continue to marvel that my sister fit into that life as she so beautifully did. Love makes marvelous pathways, and it was her complete love for her husband that gave her such contentment in a life for which she had no more preparation than I had. And it was their love together that made the Farm. There was an aura of goodness, a tradition of sharing, a generosity of spirit, and there were sincere prayers both of gratitude and for guidance.

Ethel — Peggy to all her friends — was deeply lonely after Ed was gone, but she had Edith and "Little Peg," her granddaughter, with her for those remaining years. Only when it became literally impossible for her to maintain the Farm would she agree to move. By this time she was in her eighties, and frail, but still alert and always "ready to go." She and Edith moved to the little house on Van Buren, near to our home. Norman and I, and later just I alone, took them to the beach and anywhere else they wanted to go, always including our other sister, Dorothy, who was also alone and near the same age. We helped Ethel move again in a few years, this time to a retirement home nearby. Edith's daughter Delores took her mother home with her. And Ethel's last move was to the home of her adoring granddaughter, Lea, for the final years of her long life. So she was surrounded with loving care, children, and the flowers she always loved.

On the Farm, there was certainly never a sign of poverty or penury; on the contrary, this seemed always a prosperous home. But there was certainly <u>nothing</u> wasted. Ethel darned socks, and she was a master of it—those darns were as smooth as the sock itself. She cut off the toes of worn out socks to sew onto some that could be saved! And Ed wore those 'darned' socks patiently and even proudly. She made dresses for the girls out of flour sacks. She canned everything they produced on the Farm. Ed bought day-old bread, and bathroom supplies by the gross, and always worked beyond his strength. Jodie, Nancy, and I seldom had money in our pockets beyond a very small allowance—which varied from a few pennies to a quarter a week—when we were growing up. But we did have <u>things</u>, and we always had clothes, lessons, a pretty room, horses.

Ethel's grandchildren adored her and emulated her. Oddly, she was shy about expressing her love in words, but would demonstrate it richly—perhaps typically of that generation. I loved them both, admired them, and always turned to them, but I never envied them. They are no longer with us, but their imprint is forever. It was a different life style. The children at the Farm were like little brothers and sisters to me, and they still are in our very mature adulthood. I have lost track of the number of descendants from that Farm family, because they are many! I am just sorry that the more recent ones didn't have a chance to know Grammy and Grampy and all the dear aunties and uncles and The Farm. Thus this little book.

With love,
Evelyn

About the Author

Born and brought up in Corvallis, Oregon, Evelyn Whitfield has lived most of her life there, with some years away in the Philippine Islands, and ten years in Central Oregon. Her extended family has been centered in Corvallis since 1905.

Evelyn is retired from teaching, and is the author of a personal experience book, *THREE YEAR PICNIC,* about her 37 months of captivity in the Philippines during WWII, also published by Premiere Editions. Evelyn is a devoted member of her church, enjoys gardening, reading, writing, music, and being with her friends and family.

Nancy Allworth

Index

Note: *Since the names of the immediate Allworth family, and the author, are so often repeated, they have been omitted from this index. Words like "Barn," "Cows," "Horses," and "Kitchen" also appear frequently in the text and so are not indexed.*

A

Adair, John *78, 79, 90*
Airplanes *59, 165,*
Allen, Gay *44, 118, 197, 198*
Allen, Shawn *199,*
Allen, Winston *199*
Alligator *68, 69,*
Allworth, Alf *39*
Allworth, Clark *44, 118, 159, 198*
Allworth, Grandad *44, 47, 95, 100, 101, 127, 135, 147, 168, 181, 182*

Allworth, Janet *44, 219*
Allworth, Marlene *44, 184*
Allworth, Will *39, 69, 45, 160*
Alnutt Farm *25, 57, 87, 90, 103, 113, 114, 144, 166*
Apartment *79, 123, 133, 191 197*, 268, 233
Arrowheads *89*
Artichokes *173*
Attic *70- 72, 103, 192, 197, 203, 207*

B

Babies *33, 70, 85, 100, 113, 119, 121, 130, 157, 206, 214*

Bagley, Earle and Charlotte *135*
Balcony *69, 70*
Ball, Mickey *153*
Basket(s) *34, 36, 37, 107, 160, 188*
Basselin, Joe *21, 24, 25*
Battle Ground, WA *39, 127*
Bedroom *21, 47*
Beehives *63, 94*
Bees *35, 48, 62, 87, 88, 94, 156, 172, 173*
Bell *101, 147, 161, 222*
Benton County *113, 153*
Berries *92, 108, 136, 144, 172, 177, 233*
Birdbaths *30, 193*

Black Walnut *39, 69, 78, 79*
Black, Mr. and Mrs. *154*
Black Sadie *115, 116, 154*
Blackberry *25, 58, 63, 108*
Blackout *181*
Bookshelves *24, 57, 122, 208, 211*
Boots *58, 117, 156, 218*
Bouden Piano *75, 76*
Braid(s) *37, 67, 70, 121, 166*
Brass *36, 47, 77, 79*
Bread *46, 91, 195*
Breadboard *45, 93*
Breese, Lynne and John *44, 146, 150*
Breezeway *41, 46, 47, 51, 191, 196*
Briggs, Mrs. *70*
Brumfield, Kirby *44*
Buggies *53, 114, 134, 153, 154, 156*
Burright Family *163*
Butter *91, 92, 109, 110, 132, 134, 145*

C

Calapooyans *18, 89, 115*
Calaveras, Ann *88, 111*
Calves *85, 86, 91, 130*
Camp Adair *174*
Camp Fire Girls *46, 111, 132, 151, 228*
Campbell, *Flora 115, 116*
Canada *34, 89, 122*

Canning *177, 178, 191*

Carlon, Archie *44, 96, 136, 147*

Carpenter *22*

Cedar Waxwings *88, 172*

Century House Gardens *234*

Chairs *43, 53, 67, 70, 75, 77, 211*

Chicken House *40, 50, 88, 203*

Chimney *47, 48, 71, 72*

Chipmunks *49, 69*

Christian Science Church *150*

Christmas *35, 49, 102, 118, 145, 150, 159, 181, 197, 200, 202, 204, 206, 208, 212, 214, 229,*

Churn *91,*

Climate *17, 176, 179*

Closet *48, 72, 208*

Clothes Rack *100, 101*

Clotheslines *37, 50, 78, 167*

Cocker(s) *35, 98, 99, 107, 108, 110, 135,*

Coffee Mill *45*

Collection *34, 46, 177, 185,*

College *182, 192,*

Comics *72, 162, 208,*

Cookies *46, 91, 95, 145, 146, 196, 197, 228*

Cooking *39, 46,109, 110, 118, 129, 133, 143, 145, 147-149, 211, 213*

Cooler *46,*

Copper *36, 47, 78,*

Cordell Family *183*

Cornelius, Gail and Grant *34, 47, 198, 230, 231-234*

Corvallis Gazette-Times *18, 27, 32, 108, 232*

Cousins *29,152, 198, 202, 211-215*

Cream *81, 92,*

Crest *34, 35, 111*

Crib *70, 71, 181, 207*

Cribbage *95, 191,*

Crystal Lake *125, 175*

Cub Scout *162*

Cupboard *45, 72, 96, 186,191*

D

Dairy *41, 58, 61, 91, 109, 121,
        131, 132, 161*
Damson *50, 169, 172*
Davis, Caleb *15,18, 27, 39,
        40*
Delphinium *61*
Democrat *76, 127*
Dengue, Gene *62, 79, 97*
Desk(s) *47, 75, 77, 161, 191,
        192, 195,*
Divinity *145*
Dogs *53*
Dollhouse *67, 68*
Dolls *71, 183, 191, 203, 212*
Dolly *88, 103, 113, 115, 153*
Dress-ups*191, 195, 203, 205*

E

Economy *97*
Entrance *44*
Evans, Arlyn and Celia *88,
        157*

Ewalt, Bob *157, 215, 229, 230*
Ewalt, Katherine *118, 216,
        221-223*
Ewalt, Kent *118, 221*
Ewalt, Mark*117, 118, 216,
        225*

F

Feed Sacks *80, 95*
Feet *73, 209, 222*
Fence *58, 186, 193*
Field(s) *62, 68, 84, 87, 88,
        102, 115, 209, 221,*
Filberts *75, 107, 118, 155,
        156, 166, 178,*
Fillmore Shawl *76*

Fire *47, 72, 130, 131, 132, 173, 175*
Fire Escape *23, 60*
Fireplace Mantel *33, 77, 78, 110, 144*
Fish Monger *102*
Flood *180*
Flynn, Jacklyn *181*
Forest *44, 84, 166, 197, 205, 206, 220, 234*
Frakes, Evlyn & Maurice *120-122*
Fresca *218*
Frogs *67, 87, 174*

Furnace *22, 71, 72, 107, 178, 191, 218, 219*

G

Games *57, 77, 83, 95, 127, 162, 163, 205, 210, 211*
Gamma Phi Beta *123*
Garden *63, 84, 174*
Gast, Julie *219*
Geese *35, 86, 88, 89, 174*
Gerding's Grocery *146*

Gibson, Fern *44, 77*
Glancy, Grace *147, 211,*
Glass *36, 69,*
Goats *26, 63, 79*
Goldenrod Eggs *80, 81*
Holstein *61*
Homecoming *83, 133,*
Honey *94, 95, 98,*
Horner (Museum) *24, 162*
Hornets *156*
Hutch *195, 210*

I

Ice *90, 92, 96, 178, 20,*
Ice Cream *92*
Ice Skates *90, 166, 167*
Icebox *95, 96, 101, 102*
Ingalls, Bob *118*
Inkwell *231*

J

Jacksonville, OR *127*
Japanese *134, 135, 140, 144,*
145, 165, 168, 233
Jersey Cows *61, 81*
Johansson, Delores *29, 88,*
103, 111

K

Kale *61, 62*
Kammerer (carpender) *22-*
24
Keeping Room *27, 45, 110,*
151, 210
Kindred, Jennifer *211, 213,*
214
Kindred, Kelia *35, 213*
Kindred, Kimberly *213, 230*

Kirkham, Bill *166*
Kropft, Roy *97, 132*

L

Lane *22, 36, 57, 62, 97, 113,
     125, 130, 131, 172,
     191, 196, 232*
Larson Family *25, 169*
Laundry *44, 50, 78, 79, 96,
     165, 191, 195, 202*

Lavender *50, 78, 165, 166*
Leak *97*
Lemon, E. B. *114*
LIFE Magazine *140, 208*
Loft *40, 97, 98, 100, 163, 167,
     204, 205*
Lord's Prayer *129, 182*
Louden, Edna *147*
Lundee, Gertrude *162*

Lutz, Dessa *148*
Lutz, Hank *148*
Lutz, Lea *44, 50, 70, 118,
     201, 202, 204, 210,
     214, 230*

M

Madonna *78*
Mahogany *44*
Majors, Ralph *44, 118, 148,
     183, 203*
Majors, Winston *44, 182,
     183*
Mary's Peak *144*
Mary's River *17, 25, 89, 90,
     91, 175, 180*
Mayonnaise *109, 110, 173,
     196*
Meadowland Creamery *132*
Memorial Day *175,*
Memorial Union (MU) *19,
     20, 102, 118, 120,
     144,169, 184, 215*
Memories *48, 57, 67, 95, 101,
     191, 195, 204, 212,
     213, 215, 221*
Metcalf, Cecil *230*
Metcalf, Edith *29, 36, 44, 61,
     79, 81, 91, 101, 111,
     145, 147, 198, 200,
     230*
Mice *98*
Milking *41, 58, 61, 101, 119,
     130, 131, 132 135,
     173, 183, 196*
Monks Cloth *102*
Mural *47*

Music *21, 67, 75, 76, 129, 136, 149, 150*

N

Nash, Amber *189*
Neighbor(s) *48, 90, 101, 107, 169, 187*
Neville, Charles *182, 215*
Normandy *181*

O

OAC *19, 24, 83, 114,*
Oklahoma 150
Orchard 36 49, 50, 62, 63, 85, 107, 108, 130, 156
Oregon Agricultural College *19*

Oregon Centennial *183*
Oregon State University *137, 227, 234*
Oregonian *151*
OSC *120*
Owls *49, 88*

P

Packsaddle *89*
Park Terrace *17, 21, 113, 114*
Parnell, Cindy and Patty *217, 218*
Party *183, 210, 211*
Peachtree *71, 72*
Pheasants *49, 86, 100,*
Philippine Islands*118, 123, 135, 144, 168, 184, 215, 235*
Philomath Fire Department *115*
Piano *129, 133, 191, 198, 213*
Bouden *75, 76, 211*
Ebony *75, 149, 211*
Pump Organ *75, 182, 210, 211*

Pick, Otto and Dorothy (Dot)
    30, 44, 66, 118, 123,
    125, 147, 148, 149,
    182, 189, 197, 211,
    212, 227
Pick, Shirley 141
Picket Fence 22, 36, 49, 172
Pigs 39, 69, 148
Pitchforks 78
Play Yard 47, 49, 102, 108,
    135
Playhouse 193, 197, 198, 203
Poison Oak 58, 103
Poole, Karen 221
Poplars 108, 171, 173
Porch 48, 53, 101
Portland, OR 20, 65
Prison Camp(s) 134, 140,
    233
Pump House 130, 131
Purtles 46, 110
Pussy Willows 87, 144, 145

Q

QP 88, 90, 114, 116
Quail 49, 86, 88
Quilt 139, 208

R

Rain 42, 47, 89, 117, 176,
    178, 180
Rationing 134
Refrigerator 96, 100, 101
Reimans Creamery 111
Renovation 22
Republican 76, 118, 127
Reynolds, Minerva Kiger
    152
Rhubarb 177
Ridenour, Professor 124
Rocking Horse 159
Roof(s) 42, 47, 48, 100, 177,
    209, 237
Root Beer 96
Rope 195, 204, 205, 218
Rose Bowl 227
Rosewood 44, 75
ROTC 132, 181, 184,
Rye 26
Ryecraft, Erin 217

S

Salmon Bake *184*
Sample Family *44, 72, 109*
Sawhorses *22, 101*
School *18, 47, 48, 49, 66, 111, 113, 117, 119, 123, 136, 144, 150, 161, 163, 165, 167, 169, 191, 195, 201, 211, 215, 217*
Scrapbooks *196*
Screen(s) *30, 233*
Sea Breeze *58*
Secretary *76, 77*
Sedlacek, Peggy *118, 210, 214, 217-220, 228, 229, 230*
Sheep *41, 42*
Showboat 150-152
Siebert Family *43, 44, 53, 83, 84, 90*
Sink *23, 53*
Slide *164, 165, 193, 198, 203, 204, 205*
Slough *67, 86, 174*

Snow *78, 144, 179, 180, 186, 201, 217, 218, 234*
Soap *140*
Social Security *65, 80*
Spinning Wheel *70, 79*
Stair(s) *22, 34, 68, 70, 144, 207, 233*
Starker Family *107*
Stidd Family *14, 83, 145, 159*
Stone House *18, 40, 109, 191, 196*
Stopp, Pat *231, 232*
Sunroom *233, 235*
Sunshine Club *118*
Swing(s) *204, 205*

T

Tack Room *130*
Tartar, Dr. Nick *156, 227*
Teaching *65, 182, 183*
Team *62, 97, 98, 101, 167, 186*
Telephone *21, 23, 46, 130, 179, 184*
Television *77, 210, 227*
Texas *116, 221, 229*

Thanksgiving *118*
Thistle(s) *58, 178*
Three Year Picnic 136
Toast *191, 195*
Tools *63, 66, 191*
Tuesday Club *118*
Turkeys *25, 46, 109, 146,
        148, 162, 169, 211,
        213*
Twenty-Third Psalm *129*

V

Van Vliet, Tony *49*
Vanport *180*
VICE 128, 129
Vineyard *58*

W

Wagon *97, 98*
Walker, Grampa *22, 42, 44,
        50, 52, 57, 63, 65, 67,
        73, 75, 125, 134, 149,
        191*
Walker, Kent *134*
Walker, Mary and Windy
        44, 147, 149, 150, 213
Walker, Sarah Waite *50*
Walks *49, 50*
Walls, Robert *150*
Walnuts *44, 75, 178, 184*
War(s) 33, *57, 79, 94, 111,
        122, 133, 134, 140,
        144, 149, 152, 163,
        165, 168, 233*
    WWI *19, 20, 168, 191*
    WWII *34, 37, 70, 77, 116,
        118, 130, 135, 160,
        174*
Watenpaugh, Frank *131, 162*

Watkins, Lauri *30, 44, 70, 99, 108, 109, 110, 118, 125, 157, 159, 183, 184, 185, 193, 198, 201-214, 215, 230*

Weather *178*

Wedding(s) *181, 182, 215*

Well *41, 203*

Whitby, Harris *24, 50*

Whitfield, Ray Henry and Polly *123, 135, 147*

Whitfield, Norman *44, 79, 83, 95, 108, 118, 123, 133, 134, 135, 136, 140, 144, 147, 157, 168, 184, 186, 201, 202* 210, 214, 215, *229, 290*

Wildflowers *36, 87, 90, 91,*
      115, 166
Wisteria *48, 68*
Wolfe Family *21, 44, 131,*
      174
Wood, Grandmother *182*
Wyse, Connie *217, 218*

OPPOSITE:
A page from
Peggy's Journal

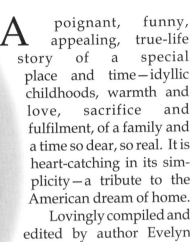

A poignant, funny, appealing, true-life story of a special place and time—idyllic childhoods, warmth and love, sacrifice and fulfilment, of a family and a time so dear, so real. It is heart-catching in its simplicity—a tribute to the American dream of home. Lovingly compiled and edited by author Evelyn Whitfield, these touching and funny recollections encompass four generations of family members and friends who shared the ambience of this wonderful place. *The Farm* begins with the Depression era, triumphs through the war years, and closes in the 70s. The setting is in the heart of Oregon's beautiful Willamette Valley, near the pretty college town of Corvallis.